I0070939

# (Buy·er List·ing)

## A **REVOLUTIONARY** APPROACH TO REAL ESTATE MARKETING AND LEAD GENERATION

Brian Inskip

Creative Force Press

*Creative Force Press*

*Buyer Listing*
© 2017 by Brian Inskip
www.MyBuyerListing.com

This title is also available as an eBook. Visit
www.CreativeForcePress.com/titles for more information.

Published by Creative Force Press
4704 Pacific Ave, Suite C, Lacey, WA 98503
www.CreativeForcePress.com

*All rights reserved. No part of this publication may be reproduced, stored in a retrieval system, or transmitted in any form or by any means--for example, electronic, photocopy, recording--without the prior written permission of the publisher.*

ISBN: 978-1-939989-26-0

Printed in the United States of America

# DEDICATION

To my Grandfather, who taught me how to think.
To my parents, who have always been there.
To my wife and kids, for being my reason.

To all those that would dare to make today better than yesterday
and have inspired me to do so.

Journey On

"*MyBuyerListing is a tool to market both sides of the coin and will change the way you play the game. If you want to shatter your sales ceiling, this is the game changer.*"
– Manda Price

*MyBuyerListing provides the perfect business cycle: it generates seller leads, makes raving fans of your buyers, and keeps you top of mind among the public as the "agent who does more."*
– Nate Evans

My
**Buyer Listing**

Get more great tools, tips, insights and supplemental materials for this book by visiting MyBuyerListing.com/blog.

# TABLE OF CONTENTS

# FOREWORD
By Adam Hergenrother

A decade ago, I entered the real estate industry as an agent, actively seeking opportunities and making whatever sacrifices necessary along the way. Through pursuing and nurturing relationships with some of the industry's top leaders, I have learned much about entrepreneurship and building successful businesses. Their wisdom helped push me along the path from novice agent to become the owner of five companies, including one of the top real estate teams in the country with over 200 agents and associates.

One of the most important philosophies I developed upon listening to the successes of my mentors, and one that informs each decision I make, involves the interconnectedness of your personal and professional lives. Your business is nothing more than a conduit for your personal growth. If you build a big business, then you'll also build a big life. Freedom lies at the core of this philosophy; freedom on how, where, when, and with whom we choose to spend our time. The most successful entrepreneurs know that effective use of their time results in more profit, and perhaps more importantly, the ability to transform more lives and live a life without limits.

The biggest challenge in real estate contributing to a lack of freedom is the amount of time agents spend prospecting or converting potential clients. For most Realtors®, the best way to achieve their highest profitability is to reduce the amount of time spent haphazardly prospecting, instead directing their attention and skills on focused, proven prospecting strategies and closing sales.

This is exactly the challenge that Brian Inskip took on: he directly applied the philosophy of freedom to his real estate career and created a system that allows agents to invest most of their efforts on income-producing activities, namely leveraging buyer listings. In *Buyer Listing: A Revolutionary Approach to Real Estate Marketing and Lead Generation*, Brian not only identifies the solution, but introduces you to the model he created, and does so in a refreshing, engaging manner. He lays out specific scripts and strategies that will only result in increasing your profit margins, while simultaneously reducing the amount of time spent achieving those results.

Few people have the comprehensive background in real estate that Brian does. Beginning at a young age, Brian assisted his family in rental property management. He then moved into the construction industry and finally transitioned into real estate, where his well-rounded knowledge of the home buying and selling process has shot him into the top 7% of his board in just a few years' time. Now, as founder of MyBuyerListing.com, he continues to climb within his own local market and stand out as an innovator nationally.

I met Brian after I had been stuck in an airport for 12 hours, flew through a lightning storm, and taught a leadership class on two hours of sleep. But despite the exhausting circumstances and the ensuing caffeine haze, Brian stood out to me even then as a leader, and as someone who was relentlessly growth oriented.

Brian's book should be a staple on the bookshelves of real estate agents, whether they be 20-year veterans, or brand new to the business. Brian has committed years to researching, testing, and building a platform for others to follow, and his personal achievements speak to the effectiveness and value his model brings. Read Brian Inskip's book, and you, too, can create a life of freedom.

Adam Hergenrother
Founder & CEO of Hergenrother Enterprises
South Burlington, VT

*Adam Hergenrother is an accomplished and well respected entrepreneur, trainer and business leader. Adam Hergenrother Companies, which includes one of the top real estate teams in the country, is fueled by Adam's commitment to thinking big and never giving up. Adam is passionate about teaching others how to harness the power of the mind to achieve a life without limits. His influence can be found throughout this book wherever bigger thinking is applied.*

*Learn more about Adam Hergenrother at AdamHergenrother.com.*

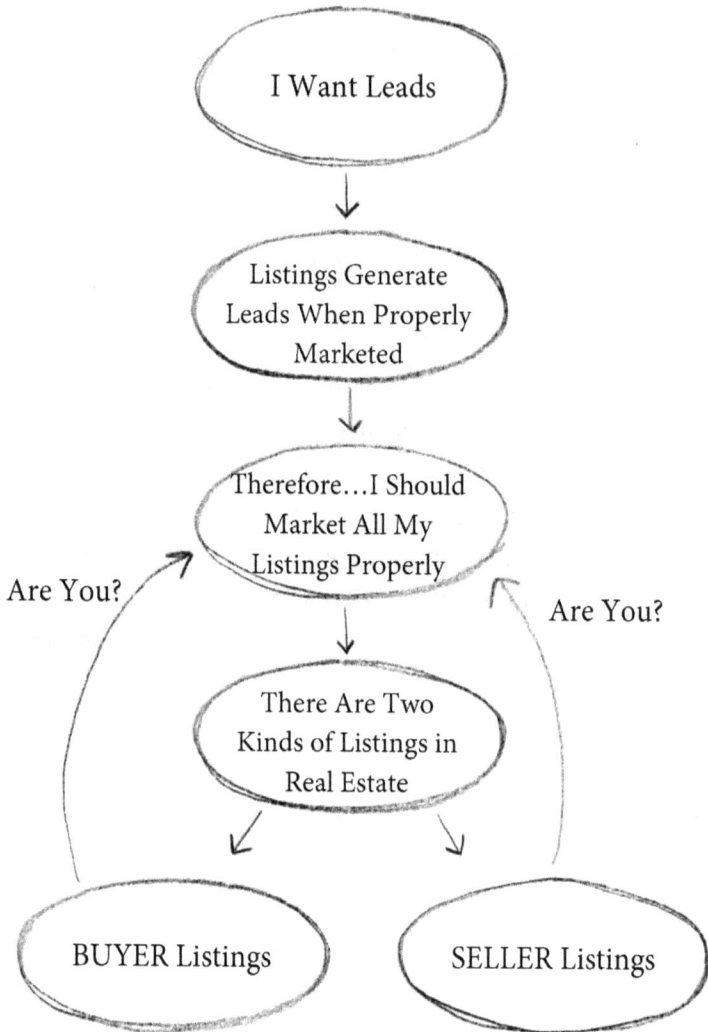

I Want Leads

↓

Listings Generate Leads When Properly Marketed

↓

Therefore...I Should Market All My Listings Properly

Are You?

Are You?

↓

There Are Two Kinds of Listings in Real Estate

BUYER Listings

SELLER Listings

Better thinking about Buyer Listings – Mind Map

MyBuyerListing.com/agent-info

# INTRODUCTION

The thing I've heard most while talking, training and masterminding with thousands of real estate agents across the country is, "I need more listings."

It's no secret that listings are the lifeblood of a successful, profitable and leveraged real estate business.

It's also no secret that it's not *more listings for listings sake*. What we really want is a better life, better opportunities and a better business.

I actually had more listings: *Buyer Listings.* I simply wasn't utilizing them.

Listings provide a presence in the marketplace, vast marketing and prospecting opportunities and consumer inquiries just to name a few benefits.

While the real estate industry has come to grips with this fact and most real estate agents agree on the importance of listings, most remain under the impression that seller listings are the only ones providing these benefits.

That is why I wrote this book.

It's vital that you understand there are in fact two types of listings you can leverage to generate massive amounts of opportunities in the most efficient way possible: Seller listings and Buyer Listings.

In this book I will introduce you to the fundamental strategies, systems and models you can apply to turn your *Buyer Listings* (home buyer clients) into marketable listings in as little as five minutes a month. By doing so, your Buyer Listings will replicate many of the same benefits that seller listings provide.

The result of this is massive. With Buyer Listings representing 50 percent of all real estate transactions, you effectively double your marketable listing inventory by applying the concepts outlined in this book.

As a Top-Producing Agent, I discovered this blind spot in my own business when I sat down and asked myself a question; a question posed by Gary Keller's best-selling book, *The One Thing*.

*"What's the one thing I need in my business such that by doing it will make everything else easier or unnecessary?"*

As I sifted through all the possibilities, the clear winner was... you guessed it...more listings.

When I asked the next phase of the question, my whole world changed:

*"What's the one thing I need to do to have more listings such that by doing it will make everything else easier or unnecessary?"*

Clearly the right answer would be something like call more For Sale by Owners, call more expireds, door knock, a new direct mail campaign, or implement some other traditional strategy used to generate listings, right?

As I dug deep into the question and allowed myself to freely explore all the possible solutions, I made a startling discovery.

I actually already had more listings...*Buyer* Listings. I simply wasn't utilizing them.

When I discovered that by shifting the way I thought about buyers and the marketing opportunities they represent, I produced much the same result from each of my Buyer Listings that my seller listings did.

I already had these *Buyer Listings* and simply wasn't tapping into their full potential. This was going to be the most efficient way to "have more listings" and grow my real estate business.

The results were astounding. Prior to this discovery, my entire team closed 70 transactions (buyer and seller) in our best year. Not bad!

After implementing the buyer marketing strategies outlined in this book, I *personally* sold 70 seller listings in just seven months. Stunning.

When I ask agents if they'd like to double their listing inventory, the answer is always a resounding *yes!* So now, I will ask you that question.

Would you like to double your listing inventory?

My hope is to show you that accomplishing this goal can be far easier than you've previously imagined...if you're willing to shift the way you look at home buyers and the marketing opportunities they represent.

I've experienced firsthand how applying the models outlined in the following chapters can dramatically increase your real estate production and profitability. I've shared these strategies with agents across the country. Now, it's your turn.

If you have any doubts about what a buyer listing is and how it applies to your business, don't worry. That's what this book is all about.

Each chapter has an activity at the end to assist you in learning this information *and* how to apply it for amazing results.

What happens in your life is the most exciting part, however, because that's really what business is all about!

I hope you'll be both inspired and empowered by what you discover throughout this book and I can't wait to hear your success stories.

Enjoy!

Brian Inskip
Founder, MyBuyerListing.com

# ACTIVITY

On a Scale of 1-10, rate the effectiveness of your current Buyer Listing campaign:

1 = I don't have one
10 = I generate at least one new piece of business for every buyer

    1     2     3     4     5     6     7     8     9    10

*If you were anything other than a 10, I would invite you to schedule a FREE STRATEGY SESSION to see how you can quickly move to a 10. Visit MyBuyerListing.com/agent-info to schedule.

# Chapter 1

# WHY?

*"There are two great days in a person's life - the day we are born and the day we discover why."* –William Barclay

*"He who has a why to live for can bear almost any how."*
– Friedrich Nietzsche

To get this party started let's begin with the most important thing: Why?

Why, out of all the things I could have done with my time, did I spend the time, energy and money to write this book?

Why would you want to invest your precious time, energy and money to read this book in its entirety?

Why would you care about applying what you'll learn from this book?

You see, without a compelling reason, your WHY, there is no need for change, no drive to dream and no reason to act, think or be any different than we are right now. There would be no need to learn anything new or become better today than we were yesterday. There would be no need for greater efficiency, better plans and strategies, or more purposeful action.

Without a WHY, the status quo will do just fine.

No one randomly sets out to change any of those things. It starts only with having some type of burning inside for something different our life. Changing what we do and how we think comes from the necessity of some other greater desire or need.

Sometimes it is conscious, obvious. *"I've had it. I can't do this anymore."* The understanding of what we want to change and why is clear. In this case, signs and symptoms that we simply cannot ignore or tolerate any longer stare us in the face. *"My doctor said if I don't quit smoking, I'll die within two years..."*

> Without a WHY, the status quo will do just fine.

In my experience, it's often much more subtle than that. There's no punch in the gut, no writing on the wall. Instead a slight dissatisfaction or yearning that we can't quite put a finger on creeps in, but we know something's not quite right.

*"What is missing?"*
*"Can I find a better way?"*
*"Is there more?"*
*"Is there a grander purpose?"*

At that moment of dissatisfaction, we have an opportunity: make a decision that will alter the trajectory of our lives, or smother the flame to stay safe and comfortable. Sadly, often times this decision isn't based on what our heart and soul truly desires, but what life experience has conditioned us to believe is (or isn't) possible.

Without intentionally exploring the things burning inside of us, our subconscious automatically suppresses these pesky thoughts of change. Your subconscious never wants to rock the boat. It makes decisions based on past experiences, outside influences and perceived safety concerns. Letting your subconscious mind run your life and your past experiences dictate your present and future is the surest way to ensure nothing in your life ever changes for the better.

Part of you is hungry for something more…something better. Since you're reading this book, you've decided to answer its pangs.

I believe this desire lives deep inside everyone, somewhere, no matter how successful they may already be, what mountains they've climbed or what lonely valley life seems to have sentenced them to.

Before we take on the work necessary to push through the barriers of change standing between you and better, you've got to have a great reason; a great WHY.

## My WHY

I'll start by sharing my WHY for writing this book. Perhaps it will help you discover yours.

For me, this January day started much like any other. I woke up, put on my tattered jeans and work boots, grabbed a cup of coffee, jumped in my truck and was out the door in under five minutes to begin my hour long commute to our jobsite in Charleston, Illinois. Up until a few months before there had never been a day in my life that I didn't enjoy working. I just like to work…always have. Being productive, serving people and creating things gives me a sense of satisfaction in life. I was just a few months away from completing a five-year apprentice program as a union pipefitter.

I absolutely loved the work. We got to play with all the big-boy toys: cut, grind and weld on steel, use cranes and move equipment larger than my house at times. The edginess of the work was exciting, as well as the craftsmanship and attention to detail.

Over the last few months though, my enthusiasm waned. For the first time in my life, I hated going to work. I hated being at work. I hated driving an hour each way to get there. Most of all, I hated myself for tolerating it.

As I cruised down I-57, loathing my life, I could not have predicted the collision that was about to take place and how it would dramatically, forever alter the course of my life.

> I could not have predicted the collision that was about to take place.

Hold back your gasp. There's no need to brace yourself for a story about a head-on automobile accident and near-death experience that led to an ultimate awakening. Fortunately, my collision that day did not involve an automobile accident, and to be honest, I'm not sure even that would have been enough of a jolt to affect the type of change my life desperately needed.

Normally, on the trip down I would be listening to WIXY, my favorite country radio station, playing the same songs day after day. In fact it had become a soundtrack of my victim mentality and resentment regiment.

Today was different though. I wasn't listening to the radio that morning. My cousin, Jason, had given me a CD series by Jim Rohn entitled *The Challenge to Succeed* (you can watch one of my favorite clips on my BLOG at MyBuyerListing.com/blog). Certainly it wasn't my normal cup of tea, or coffee in my case. In fact, I had never listened, read, experienced or given the slightest care to any sort of motivational, inspirational or personal development anything...ever. It didn't fit my "persona" (genius, I know).

Nonetheless, as I cruised down the interstate and listened to the words of a man I had never met I felt myself getting more and more drawn in. He had a very simple birds and bees way of discussing the complexities of life and business, success and happiness. It was all making perfect sense to me. I would smile here and there, as he was not only brilliantly insightful but humorous in just the right measure.

Yes, it was refreshing and I was enjoying myself, and for a few moments my woes seemed to wash away and then...BOOOOM! I got blindsided – punched right in the gut and never saw it coming.

As Mr. Rohn shared his own story of a low point in his life and the victim stance he had adopted as to why things hadn't worked out better, he began to share his story of *the day that turns your life around.*

His words hit me like I had crossed over the median and met a semi, head on.

In an instant I felt the entire weight of my life crash down on my shoulders.

All the heartbreaks I had successfully buried and hid away started simultaneously tugging at my heart strings nearly ripping it to pieces.

Yes, this was a collision.

Next, Jim Rohn came across the speakers in my beat up Chevy truck and spoke these words:

*"For things to change for you, you have to change."*

In that moment, I had my first encounter with full responsibility for all my life had been, what it was and what it would ever become.

I pulled off the interstate, overwhelmed with the weight of the radical paradigm shift that had just taken place and the realization that all the crap in my life that pissed me off and I blamed on other people was actually *on me*. The scapegoat, my refuge from taking responsibility for my life and its outcomes, vanished and left me totally exposed.

Then, I cried. Yep, I balled like a baby right there on the side of the interstate.

Twenty-seven years of life experience, failure, disappointment and regret came crashing down on me, and trust me there was plenty.

But, having the responsibility fall squarely on me was not the heaviest part. Sure, feeling the weight of my past was heavy, but it was nothing compared to the weight of my future. Regrets about my past and disappointment about my current station in life were obvious. The real weight I felt was in knowing with absolute certainty, and for the first time that my future was 100 percent my responsibility, and suddenly I felt compelled to do something extraordinary with it.

> It was simultaneously debilitating and liberating.

I think the reason this experience was so profound was that it was simultaneously debilitating and liberating. I was the only one responsible for all the shortcomings and dissatisfaction in my life. At the same time, it was liberating to realize that I am in complete control of my destiny and nothing is off limits.

### Accepting the Way it Is

Here is the kicker. Even though I was terribly dissatisfied with my life up to that point, I was still okay with it. While I may not have liked it and even despised it, I had come to grips that at least for the foreseeable future, this was my life and I wasn't inclined to do anything to change it. I didn't even *realize* I had the power to do so.

Without a college education, without seeing myself as overly intelligent or skilled in any particular area, and without having a clear sense of purpose, I was prepared to re-live the same day over and over.

If Jason hadn't shared that CD with me, I'm quite certain my life would look nothing like it does now, and exactly the same as what it was back in 2011. Jason, if you're reading this book, thank you for having the courage and compassion to share that CD with me despite feeling hesitant to do so, wondering if people would "make fun" of you for engaging with that kind of *hokey pokey, self-help jargon.*

I hope you, too, will find a breakthrough in this book that compels you to create a new trajectory for your life and business. I hope you decide to take ultimate responsibility for every aspect of your life and your business, making the most of every day so that someday when you reflect back on your life you'll have no regrets.

Then, after your breakthrough take it a step further and do what Jason did for me: share it with someone else.

You never know what's going on inside a person and how sharing one spark may ignite what they've secretly yearned for and their life is forever changed for the better. It's an amazing gift we all have the power to give, every day.

### Changing Our Thinking Allows Everything to Change

Now, that day on the interstate, everything about me did *not* instantaneously change. I didn't suddenly become the type of person who could accomplish all of the things I've done since that day up to the time of writing this book. But my thinking shifted in that moment which has *allowed* everything to change. What did instantaneously change was me deciding to take ownership and responsibility for my life. In that moment I took the first step on an amazing journey; a journey you can also decide to embark on right now.

After that day I was searching for *more*—whatever that was, I wasn't sure of yet—and was amazed at how *more* started to reveal itself in my life.

Within a few weeks I quit my $37/hour union job with benefits and started my real estate career as an independent agent with Keller Williams. I had no business background, no client database, no college degree, no marketing experience, and really nothing that would be considered the makings of a successful real estate agent.

And did I mention it was 2011? The market was tanked in the midst of the worst recession since the Great Depression.

All I had was a commitment to do something more with my life and a willingness to take full responsibility for it.

The next few years were transformative as I embarked on a journey of personal development, business training and un-locking potential I never knew I possessed.

**Testing Intentions**

The beginning of the journey was rocky, as it can often be when you're making big shifts in your life.

About six months in with only one closing and nearly all of our savings depleted, I began to doubt that I could make this work. Was it possible that I had made one of the worst decisions of my life?

The stakes were even higher now because my wife and I brought our first child into the world four months after I quit my secure union job. Now I was supporting a family of three and the money to pay bills was running out, fast.

I almost allowed fear and doubt to win…almost.

With a determination from somewhere deep inside me I kept going, I kept learning. Anytime there was training available I showed up like a sponge, fully engaged. Then, I took the most important step of learning something new: I went out and applied what I had learned.

> Was it possible that I had made one of the worst decisions of my life?

### Building Infrastructure

My Team Leader, Manda (who was also a key influence in making the jump into real estate), told me about an eight-week course coming to our area designed to develop the mindset, skills and accountability needed to make dramatic shifts in life and business.

It was a course called B.O.L.D. by MAPS training (check them out at MAPS.com) and the cost was $800 dollars.

Remember, at this point I had no money coming in, our savings was all but gone and I was contemplating conceding that I was not cut out for real estate. Maybe the miserable life I'd liberated myself from a few months prior was really all I was able to offer my family.

Jim's words spoke to me again:

*"For things to change for you, you have to change."*

> For things to change for you, you have to change.

It wasn't the system, the business or anything else keeping me from what I wanted, it was *me*.

I decided to give it one last chance and wrote the check in full for my B.O.L.D. tuition, leaving less than three digits in my bank account. I decided to completely surrender myself to the process and promise of B.O.L.D.

Eight weeks later I had built up a substantial listing inventory and put more homes under contract than I had in the previous seven months combined! On the last weekend of the training I had three offers, for three of my listings, spread out on my desk and negotiating all of them to a sale in one day. Then, all three of those sellers went out and bought new homes with me that same weekend! Six sales in one weekend! At that point I knew this real estate thing was going to work out...

B.O.L.D. harnessed my desire, directed it to purposeful action and equipped me with the strategies and skills to make it a reality.

About nine months after starting in real estate and building on the momentum I created in B.O.L.D. I hired my first team member: an administrative assistant. A few months later I added a buyer's agent, and by the end of my second full year in real estate, we had reached the top 7 percent in our market in closed production.

As I write this book, I am now celebrating a new milestone: having personally sold over 60 seller listings during the last six months in my fifth year of real estate sales.

It's been a process. While I didn't produce the results of a Top Producing agent overnight, I did take the first step on the journey. Then the next, and the next.

No one could have taken that step for me, and no one can take it for you.

No one could give me the desire to want more from life. No one can give it to you. People can absolutely help you discover your desire, as Jim Rohn and countless others have done for me, but it's important to know that ultimately it's something that comes from inside of you. Own it, embrace it and let it flow out!

It wouldn't have been possible without all of the amazing people I've met along the way sharing their secrets, strategies and support. Learning from those already doing what you want to achieve is one of the single greatest tools to get where you want to go faster and with far fewer obstacles.

It also wouldn't have been possible, especially in five short years, without amazing systems and models to follow.

And that is my WHY for writing this book. Perhaps you are in a place where you feel trapped by the circumstances of your life and business. Or, maybe you are unknowingly like I was, feeling just *okay* enough with the status quo to tolerate it, missing out on the life that deep down inside somewhere, you truly desire. Maybe you're already wildly successful (by most standards) and have already woken up to the reality that you control your own destiny. If this is the case, then you probably already know the importance of daily reminders and have already committed to a journey of continued growth and learning.

Wherever you are now, this book will help you discover and find the desire to see how much further you can go.

In the pages that follow expect to find strategies and systems that can take your real estate business and life to a whole new level. I say *can* because it's up to you to shift your thoughts, learn and take hold of them and put them into practice.

You will have the opportunity to learn my best practices which have allowed me to maximize my production (selling nearly four times as many homes as typical agents) while working less than 40 hours a week.

You will learn simple methods to apply those practices to your own business.

The strategies come from study, experience and development of how to get the most out of the time energy and investments you make in your business.

Next it's up to you to unleash your desire to create more, have more and become more.

It's up to you to take the first step on the journey and apply what you will learn. You'll have my full encouragement and support along the way.

Step one starts with your thinking. The things I will share may very likely challenge traditional thinking and approaches to how to operate your real estate business.

So, be ready to keep an open mind and to explore a new perspective.

I can assure you that every strategy I share is based on real estate fundamentals that have always been at the helm of being a successful agent. The difference is these fundamentals have evolved into the hybrid strategies you will discover inside.

# Activity: Your WHY

To start forming your WHY around reading this book and implementing Buyer Listings into your business, let's explore some of the benefits.

1) Enter the number of buyers you closed in the last year or you plan to close this year: _____ (A)

Enter your average commission: X $_____ (B)

Level 1 opportunity cost of Buyer Listings = _____(C)

2) What would you do if you had an additional _____ (enter value from line C) in income in the next 12 months?

3) List three other people in your life that would benefit from your increased income and how:

  1) Name:
  Benefits:

  2) Name:
  Benefits:

  3) Name:
  Benefits:

## Chapter 2

# WHY BUYER LISTINGS?

Let's start by defining what a *Buyer Listing* is. If I ask this question to a room full of 100 real estate agents I tend to get 100 different answers. The proper understanding of what a Buyer Listing is and what it can do for your business isn't well-known.

I'm going to give you my definition; a definition of a concept that will bring greater leverage and profitability to your business.

## (buy · er list · ing)

noun

 REAL ESTATE

 a *marketable display* of homebuyers' search criteria that when properly marketed *generates leads.*
 "buyer listings carry the same marketing and lead generation opportunities as Seller Listings when you have the right systems and strategies."

The question is, do your home buyers currently fit this definition? Do you have their home search criteria in a marketable display that you can send to someone just as easily as you can send your newest seller listing link? Are your *Buyer Listings* generating leads for you?

If the answer is no, you probably still have buyers in your business…just not Buyer Listings.

Don't worry if not, it's not a problem it's an opportunity and the sole purpose of this book is to help you capitalize on it.

Hopefully in the last chapter you were able to connect or reconnect with whatever it is that makes you excited to get up every day and live a life you love. By this I don't mean everyday will be sunshine and roses, but your WHY helps you take on life's challenges with a clear understanding of why you're doing it.

Inspiration and motivation are a critical piece of creating anything. The key word is a *piece*...

Have you ever been super amped up about something or set a new goal that you knew was going to happen for you...and then it never happened? For some reason your excitement and enthusiasm alone did not magically create the result for you. What's up with that?!

Let's take a quick look at a law from physics. The inspiration and motivation you have are representative of *potential energy*. At the onset, your goals still represent an object at rest – nothing more than a collection of matter and *potential* energy.

Because we know an object at rest stays at rest and an object in motion stays in motion, we begin to see a simple truth emerge. To achieve our goals requires a force to act on that goal to put it into motion. The keyword there is *act*.

Without an action, there is no movement. All the *potential* energy in the world (wishing, wanting and hoping) won't move you an inch closer to achieving your goals.

NO ACTION

HOPE...
WISH...
WANT...
WAIT...

MASSIVE ACTION

...INEFFECTIVE

MASSIVE ACTION

...INEFFICIENT

OPTIMAL ACTION

...EFFECTIVE
AND EFFICIENT

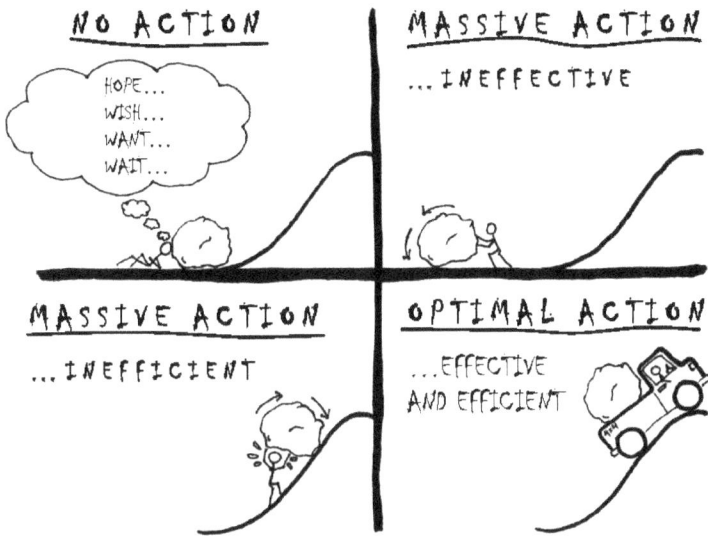

I wish I could say it was as simple as that. If you simply do *something, anything,* then you'll have everything you ever wanted, but again it's all still subject to the laws of physics. I can't expect to roll a bowling ball down the shoe rack and get a strike, so doing just *anything* will not necessarily get you to your goal.

The forces we apply to the object at rest and potential energy must create the right trajectory to arrive us at our goal. We need to understand the right path to the target.

This is commonly referred to as models and systems in the real estate industry. Models and systems are a variety of proven methods and examples that are commonly accepted to produce certain outcomes.

One of the best collections ever assembled can be found in Gary

Keller's book, *The Millionaire Real Estate Agent*.

In this book he details the models and systems (actions) used by agents producing at least one million dollars in net real estate income per year. At the time he wrote the book there were only a handful doing so. Since its publication that book has become a foundation for the industry and the number of millionaire agents has gone through the roof.

Why? Many people in the industry suddenly had the appropriate models and systems to use as a guide to *act on*, relative to their personal goals, motivation and inspiration.

In more recent years we've seen increasing examples of agents across the globe applying the fundamentals of these models and systems and evolving them to reach unprecedented levels of production.

So we can reasonably conclude that in order to achieve our goals we need more than just inspiration and motivation. *We will need strategies* that align with our aspirations and create the force necessary to end up where we want to go.

### The Curveball vs. Blockbuster

If you want to be the best pitcher in baseball you want to model the thinking of Candy Cummings who explored the boundaries of what is possible. It's to your advantage to see beyond what everyone else is doing, always looking for the gray areas between the way everyone else does it, or the way it's always been done. It's not re-inventing the wheel, but rather it's exploring and sometimes pushing the boundaries of what's possible; what's better.

Baseball gives us a prime example the first time Candy Cummings threw a curveball. No one knew what to do. Batters were totally unprepared and most did all they knew how to do: complain to the umpire and assume the rules were being broken.

In fact, no rules were broken. It was simply that Cummings was operating at a more effective level within those rules. He was operating on the same principal as all the other pitchers: *strike out the batter.* The difference was he found a better strategy by exploring the gray area, then acted on it. They even had to bring in a new catcher just to catch the most disruptive pitch in baseball.

On the flip side, let's look at Blockbuster. Once a titan in the home movie and video game retail industry, is now a burger joint in my home town.

Blockbuster navigated several industry shifts, namely the introduction of DVD's and Blu-ray.

Blockbuster dominated the movie and gaming industry for years. They successfully adapted to an evolving industry with the introduction of DVD's and similar advancements reaching its peak in 2004.

Six years later Blockbuster filed for bankruptcy.

Blockbuster failed to do the one thing every business must do: evolve.

Blockbuster's customers evolved, its competitors evolved, technology evolved, but Blockbuster failed to recognize the significance of the shift in what their customers valued. As a consequence, Blockbuster became irrelevant.

When it comes to running your real estate business, we have the same opportunities to explore the boundaries and effectiveness of what we're doing and to improve on it. Otherwise we may become a Blockbuster, quickly fading into obscurity.

Keep in mind that the fundamentals of our industry don't change. The fundamentals will always exist to provide value to your marketplace. *How* we do it and *what* the marketplace values, however, is ever-changing.

### Staying Relevant

It was that type of thinking that led me to explore the most effective ways to direct offers, messages and marketing to my marketplace in order to bring in new and repeat clientele.

I was looking for the curveball. Why? One could look at where I was and say there was no need to explore the *gray areas*. After all, after my training I had climbed into the top 7 percent in our market by the end of my second full year in real estate. My growing team was building good momentum, learning and improving every day. I was at the very point that traps a large majority of people, whether in their personal or business lives.

In comparing myself to others around me, my results were pretty phenomenal. From that vantage point there was no need to do anything different.

That was the wrong thought process.

When I asked myself another question posed by Gary Keller in his best-selling book, *The One Thing*, I got a totally different answer:

*"Are you doing it the best you can do, or the best that it can be done?"*

I decided to take on a much bigger vision for my life and business in large part because of that book…but it also created a problem…

*Good enough* may have worked for the mediocre visions I had, but it certainly didn't pass muster as *the best it could be done*. But how could I do more? I still only had the same 24 hours in a day.

### Breakthrough

Then, a wonderful thing happened! Born out of necessity to find more efficient, profitable and productive ways of doing things, I started exploring what I was doing. My mind began to open up, actively exploring all the ways to improve the results I was producing without needing more time.

One day that searching paid off in a big way. It hit me: there are two types of listings in my real estate business (buyers and sellers) and I was really only treating one of those as an asset.

Like nearly every agent in the country I spent my time marketing seller listings to get a home sold and if done properly, generate additional leads from having that "asset" out in the marketplace.

After all, that's how it's always been done, right?

But what about the other half? What about the buyers?

We're in a time where data is becoming more and more valuable. Companies invest and spend heavily, pouring over data collecting and storage because they know how much time, money, energy and failure it can save!

> The home buyers we work with to find the right home carry the same marketing and return potential as the seller listings we market.

You are about to discover how that same opportunity exists in your real estate business when you start looking at buyers a little differently.

What had dawned on me was this: the home buyers we work with to find the right home carry the same marketing and return potential as the seller listings we market.

*That's right, you can market your buyers*, much like you would a seller listing and open up a whole new world in your real estate business…and it's a big world!

Learning the strategies and philosophies about Buyer Listing Marketing in the coming pages will not only make your world bigger, it's more *profitable*, more *productive*, more *enjoyable* and my personal favorite…*simpler*.

Many agents are unfamiliar with this concept or think that when I say *buyer listing marketing* I'm referring to a methodology of generating more buyer leads. That couldn't be further from the truth. To see real-time examples of how agents across the country use buyer listings to attract sellers in a very powerful way, take a few moments right now to check out MyBuyerListing.com/agent-info.

Then, open the next chapter and watch your business potential expand.

## Chapter 3

# THE PHYSICS OF BUYER LISTINGS

Remember in the opening chapter when we talked about the importance of having a compelling WHY or reason to do something?

Let's take a closer look at why having a buyer marketing campaign works and what you're missing out on if you don't have one.

Let's start by looking at the real estate industry basics. In 2015 there were over 5.4 million existing home sales in the United States alone. Naturally, *each of those sales had both a seller and a buyer,* which brings the total to nearly 11 million considering the two sides for each home sold.

Over the years, the real estate industry has gained an undeniable understanding of how marketing seller listings generates additional business opportunities. In Gary Keller's book *The Millionaire Real Estate Agent* he gives a detailed analysis of how for every properly marketed seller listing, an agent should expect to produce at least one additional piece of closed business.

This could come from a variety of sources, whether it be people you meet at open houses, sign calls, online inquiries, neighborhood calls, referrals, etc.

The problem is most agents have only figured out how to utilize half of those two sides (seller listings) as effective tools to generate additional business. HALF, only 50 percent – not even a majority. If you fall into the vast majority of agents who don't have an effective Buyer Listing marketing system, then you fall into the vast majority only getting a return on half of your assets.

When you decide to employ the concepts of this book and look at buyers differently you will extend this opportunity to all of your buyer sides as well. Or to put it another way, *for every Buyer Listing you market properly, you should expect to produce at least one additional closed piece of business.*

> For every Buyer Listing you market properly, you should expect to produce at least one additional closed piece of business.

## By The Numbers

I think we could all agree that 50 percent in just about anything is not a winning percentage…at least not when a much higher percentage is readily available to you. I'm assuming that because you're reading this book, you're like me. You want your business to be running as close to 100 percent productivity and efficiency as possible.

So what does that look like with Buyer Listings? Let's take a look at a business without Buyer Listings, then see what happens when we add the strategies discussed throughout this book.

Let's say you have a real estate business that closed 100 sales in the previous year. And of those 100 sales, 50 percent were through working with buyers.

## Closed Sales with No Buyer Listings

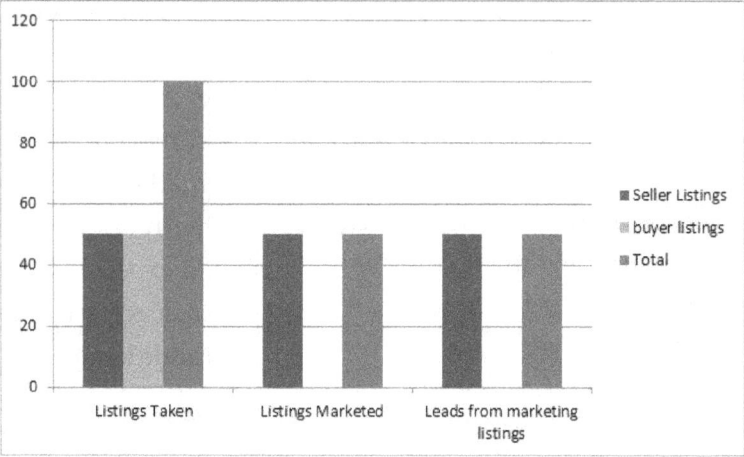

## Closed Sales with Buyer Listings

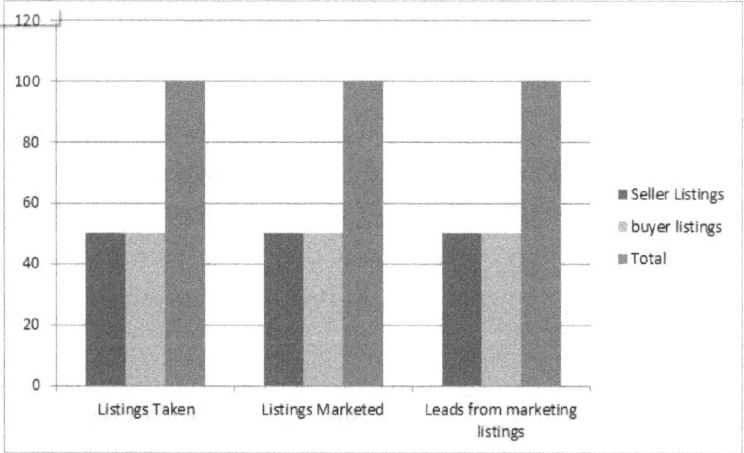

As you can see from the graph, some really interesting things happen when you introduce Buyer Listings.

First, the obvious. When you advertise your buyers' needs, you attract more sellers (much the same way marketing seller listings attracts buyers). An entirely new set of seller listing leads come to you because of marketing your buyers.

> By introducing Buyer Listings, you create a full cycle that continually feeds and grows your business.

The second impact is more indirect but just as powerful. The graph shows a 50 percent increase in closed buyers over the same 12-month period. How? This is because you generated additional buyer leads from all those extra seller listings. You will also see an increase in buyer lead conversions when you can offer this as a value-added service.

The third is perhaps the most exciting. As you project this graph out further and further you'll continue to see exponential increases. How? Because by introducing Buyer Listings, you're actually creating a FULL CYCLE that continually feeds and grows your business.

The seller leads generate buyer leads, which you then re-market and generate additional seller leads with. In turn, you market those sellers and generate yet more buyer leads to market for even more seller leads. Do you see how this cycle never ends?

# A Full-Cycle Real Estate Business

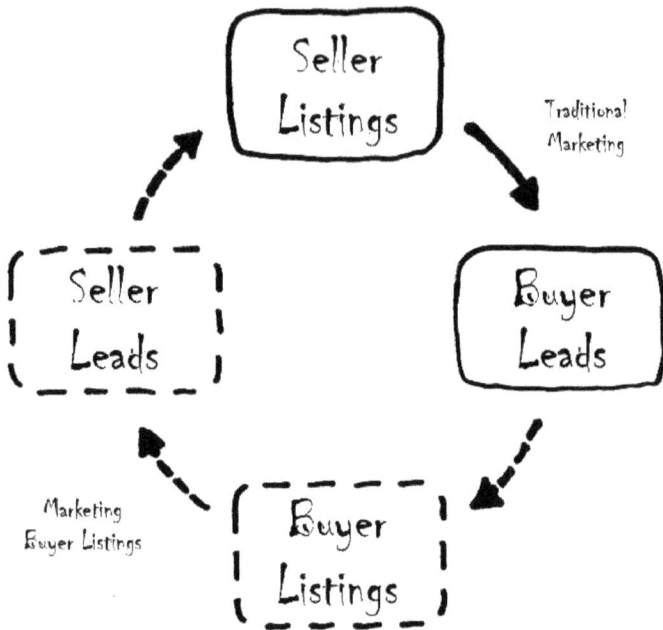

Seller Listings

Traditional Marketing

Buyer Leads

Seller Leads

Marketing Buyer Listings

Buyer Listings

Now that you see how the cycle works, is this a result you would like to see in your own business?

Let's face it, like I mentioned earlier, wanting and wishing for something or being inspired or motivated won't be enough to turn it into reality.

Action is what's needed, and not just any action, the *right* action. This means you'll need the strategies, models and systems.

## The Hammer and the Nail

There is an important question that typically comes up by this point that I want to address.

*Why, with all the benefits Buyer Listings provide, haven't I heard of this before?*

It comes down to the hammer and the nail.

Imagine two objects, a *hammer* and a *nail.*

If I were to ask you to go out and frame a house with only a box of nails, you would have quite the task in front of you.

Can you imagine trying to drive nails into 2x4's with just your hand? Perhaps impossible and inefficient at best, with this approach it wouldn't be long before you gave up or began seeking out alternatives.

Likewise if I only gave you the hammer and again asked you to frame a house you would face the same challenge of being ill-equipped for the task at hand.

You see, without the hammer, the nail is useless and likewise, without the nail the hammer is useless.

Your Buyer Listings are the nail. They have always been there, much like the box that's probably sitting around collecting dust somewhere in your garage. What's been missing is the hammer that allows us to drive the nails in order to build something.

> **Without the hammer, the nail is useless.**

In other words, without an efficient and effective means to market your Buyer Listings (the hammer) it made more sense to pursue alternative means to grow your business.

MyBuyerListing.com is the hammer (really more like a high-powered nail gun) allowing you to quickly and efficiently put your Buyer Listings to use.

And that's exactly what I'll be getting into in the next chapters.

## Exercise

Stop…take the next 60 seconds and look around you wherever you are and write down everything you see.

_____

_____

_____

_____

_____

Now, look at your list. How many of the items didn't exist 5, 10 or 15 years ago? Write the number next to each item of when it was invented or significantly evolved.

Lastly, circle each item that has evolved in the last five years.

If your list is like mine, there won't be many things around you that haven't significantly evolved or at one point in the recent past didn't even exist.

Even those that appear on the surface to have escaped the wheels of evolution have probably seen a fair share of progress in manufacturing, marketing, distributions, inventory management size, efficiency of use, and business automation.

Progress and evolution happens with or without us. The key for us is to keep pace.

## Chapter 4

# SHORT FUSE VS. ETERNAL FLAME

I've thrown a lot at the wall to see what sticks in my life, and particularly in my real estate business.

I remember the first homebuyer seminar I taught with a whopping turnout of two...in an entire hotel conference room with a catered lunch (luckily, I had won the event venue in a drawing so the losses were minimal).

I remember the kickoff cookout I hosted when I first got into real estate. Everyone in my database was invited, which at that time consisted of our wedding guest list. Considerably more people from that list showed up to our wedding than my cookout.

I remember sitting in a dunk tank in the front yard of an open house...yes, you heard that right. I knew I was in for a long day when the tank arrived late, meaning the water wouldn't have time to warm up. That sweet, innocent-looking little girl walked straight up to the trip lever and proceeded to manually trigger my first frosty plunge, followed by four more consecutive dunks until she'd had her fill. Ugh.

Perhaps my favorite was walking 45 miles in a blizzard at below zero temperatures to raise $20,000 for under-privileged youth to attend a youth leadership program.

I've never been afraid to try things. For me, that was the quickest way to figure out if it was going to work or not and far less painful than getting bogged down analyzing all the things I *could* do, yet never do anything.

I never went into things blind though. Everything I've done over the years has had a foundation of proven, time-tested fundamentals.

When you try a lot of things, the clear winners start to emerge. When they do, you double down and do more of it. Then, continue the process until you see a shift in results. When you find yourself spinning your wheels on something that isn't working, simply take your foot off the gas and try something else.

There are a few key things I've found that constitute a winner for me. You may have different ones, but I wanted to share mine in hopes it will help you identify your own key criteria to define a winner.

For me, the first key when it comes to business is that *it must produce a measurable result* worthy of the investment made: time, money, energy or a combination.

With limited hours and resources to invest, you have to have accountability.

When you really love what you do though, be careful. If you absolutely love showing people houses, you may get a lot of joy from the work that you do. But at the end of the day are you struggling to pay your annual MLS dues?

You may knowingly be showing homes to unqualified buyers or

ones who haven't committed to you, because at the end of the day, you just enjoy it.

Don't get me wrong, it's critical to enjoy what you do. You'll never reach your full potential if you're doing something you despise and aren't passionate about. But passion has to be mixed with accountability for positive results.

You deserve to enjoy what you do *and* enjoy the fruits of your labor. If you're working with the right clients, they wouldn't want you to be struggling, missing family time or being stressed out. If not, you're working with the wrong people and you definitely deserve better than that.

It doesn't have to be either or: either enjoying what you do and serving people at a high level, or having a fruitful real estate career.

> Passion must be mixed with accountability for positive results.

No, it's *both*. You can have both and you deserve both. Hold your activities and investments accountable for results.

This leads me to my second key: anything I do has to be something I enjoy or have passion about. Now, there will certainly be times when you don't love every little task you do or it may be a bit more indirect, but in general, you should enjoy the things you're doing on a daily basis.

This is one reason why I love Buyer Listings so much. I enjoy calling people about them and I enjoy the atmosphere it creates with the people I talk to. It's not a hard sales approach, but rather comes from wanting to contribute something meaningful to others. It also feeds my energy to know that people are interested and appreciate what I'm sharing with them.

I love how it's made many of the other activities, like calling FSBO's, expireds and circle prospecting more fruitful in results and more enjoyable. Adding Buyer Listings to your conversations has amazing ways of opening people up and building a solid relationship built on value.

> The will do's are the only ones you can count on to actually get done.

My third key is that it has to be something I *will* do, consistently, over time. Nothing beats a dynamic strategy, backed up with an efficient system implemented with consistent habits. It may sound silly to say it has to be something that I *will* do, but let's be real. We don't always do what we should and certainly aren't doing all we could. Some of the things we could do, we really shouldn't be, and some of the things we should do we just won't and don't.

It's okay to have an honest conversation with yourself, or better yet with a coach about what you are and are not willing to do out of the vast sea of things you *could* do.

Take an honest look.

The will do's are the only ones you can count on to actually get done.

To test a *should* or *could* versus a *will,* simply up the stakes a little bit. If you're getting ready to make a new commitment ask yourself if you'd be willing to send me your car's title, and if you don't end up doing what you said you would, I get to keep your car.

Typically, if I am coaching someone in this situation, the response goes something like this:

"*I can't do that, my wife would kill me if I gave away our car.*"

Do you see what is happening there? We just found a *should* disguised as a *will.* The key is to get clear on what you will do so you can let everything else go...at least for now. Write the *could* and *should* down and know you can always go back to them, but until you have the *will* to do it, it will just be a distraction taking up valuable time, energy and resources from something you'll actually do and see it through.

When it comes to selecting your daily actions think eternal flame, not just short fuse.

Short fuse implementation is short-lived and your results soon die out.

This is just as true for your life, relationships and money as it is for the messages and offers you put in front of clients.

### Connect and Communicate

In the real estate business, we're all connectors. Whether it is connecting a client with the right home, a buyer with a lender, locating a reputable contractor, or connecting someone with an opportunity, leadership and training.

We spend a lot of our time connecting problems with solutions.

The depth, quality and number of connections you make will determine your success.

Be a great connector! Then, keep the connections strong.

One of the most effective ways I have found to keep my connections strong with people is through value-based content, offers and messages.

Buyer Listings provide some of the most relevant, exclusive and value-based offers you can send to homeowners on a recurring basis…and they love it!

On any given day you and I can only communicate and connect with so many people. But when we have a great supplemental message that the people we connect with receive on a regular basis (and *want* to receive), our reach extends much further.

That's an example of the difference between being a short fuse and an eternal flame.

When you decide to become the eternal flame versus the short fuse, your entire life and business change. You'll start seeing an exponential return on your efforts because your message and offer *sticks* in people's minds. They engage with your content, and when the time comes for them to need real estate advice, they call *you*.

Buyer Listings are a tool to help you be the eternal flame and to have eternal flame content that's both efficient and relevant.

The bonus is that while many homeowners may choose to subscribe to your Buyer Marketing (receive regular updates of your buyer listings) long before they have an actual need or desire to sell, they're still in a place to refer you to more immediate movers! That is a reoccurring challenge in real estate – finding clients who need your services this week or this month.

When you, your marketing and your messages commit to being the eternal flame you no longer are subject to the stress, inefficiency and insurmountable task of having to get all of your *now* business...now.

This is a mindset shift that has been becoming more and more prevalent in real estate as the industry has become religious about its numbers. We figured out that if we talk with 20 people and only one has an immediate real estate need, having something else to offer the other 19 to increase the chances of them calling us when their need to buy or sell arrives is powerful.

## Exercise

List the best sales pitch and offers you have for buyers, sellers and people that don't have an immediate real estate need:

Buyers:

Sellers:

People with No Immediate Need:

Put yourself in their shoes and ask the following questions:

For Sellers:

How would the offer of receiving a regular update of your active buyers stack up to what you normally offer/send?

For Buyers:

How would my offer create the most opportunities for the buyer and how does it expand their home search options beyond just actively-listed properties?

For Everyone Else:

Would seeing an active list of buyers every month keep these people engaged and increase the chances that when they have a real estate need they'll call me?

## Chapter 5

# THE 3-STEP FORMULA FOR TURNING BUYERS INTO LISTINGS

I promised you models and systems in this book. I'm about to make good on that promise by giving you the very same formula I follow to market Buyer Listings and what you should expect to see in return for following the three simple steps outlined in this chapter.

Theory is not my favorite. Theory is unproven. I like working with formulas supported by evidence of successfully producing a certain result over time. We aren't dealing with theory in this book. It would be irresponsible of me (and annoying) to ask you to be a Guinea Pig for a radical new idea.

Everything you'll read are things I have personally done in my own business and have helped others do as well.

I'll start off with a real-world example from my very first experience marketing Buyer Listings. This will allow you to get the whole story, then work backwards through the specific strategies; strategies that allow you to create the same type of results, over and over again.

### The Day I Became a Believer in Buyer Listings

*I had done nearly every type of prospecting you can imagine from asking my sphere for referrals, FSBO's, expireds, door-knocking, circle prospecting, workshops, social media...you name it. At one* point I was even doing an open house seven days a week!

I'd experienced success from all of these sources and that's why it was so powerful to me to see how much easier and effective Buyer Listing marketing was the very first time I put it to use.

At the time I was 100 percent focused on listings. That's getting listings, servicing listings and selling listings. That was my bread and butter.

I had been developing the idea and strategy behind Buyer Listings for over a year and was pretty sure it would work based on everything I had learned about people, marketing and what is important to sellers. This was the knowledge base of hundreds of meetings, thousands of conversations and countless hours of learning and study.

At that point it was still theory though, and it was time to test it out; to cut the umbilical cord in a real-world situation.

We had a buyer that was looking for a home in a newer neighborhood called Ashland Park in my hometown of Champaign, Illinois.

Inventory was extremely low at the time and there were not many options available for this particular client. So, I called a past client of mine that I knew had a rental property in the area.

I told her about our buyer and described the features of the home they were looking for. At least two bedrooms up to a price of $150,000.

*"Do you know of anyone in the area that would consider selling?"* *She couldn't think of anyone at the time but said she would let me know if she thought of someone.*

*As soon as we got off the phone, I emailed her a link (using MyBuyerListing.com Buyer Listing feature) to this particular buyer's listing (their home search criteria), describing everything we had just talked about.*

*It was just like sending a link for a hot new listing to a buyer lead...and the end result was eerily similar, much to my satisfaction!*

*I kept making calls in that neighborhood and connected with another homeowner who had previously tried selling twice with no success. Not knowing what else to do, they were renting out the property while living halfway across the country.*

*In that conversation it was clear they desperately wanted to sell but had given up hope that it would be possible, and frankly had lost faith in the real estate industry's ability to get it sold.*

*I've had hundreds of conversations with homeowners in the exact same position. I'm confident that no amount of explanation of our services or marketing plan would have instilled the confidence they needed to give selling another shot at that particular time. They felt burned.*

I had something tangible to offer them, and it made all the difference.

*But...I had something tangible to offer them and it made all the difference. I shared with her that we had a buyer looking in the area and described the criteria they were searching for. It was a perfect fit. Then, I emailed them our Buyer Listing link so they could actually see it for themselves. Yes, it is a real buyer!*

*This opened their mind that selling was a real possibility and was now almost literally knocking on their door.*

*Ultimately, it was too powerful for even their past disappointment to overcome.*

*They decided to give it a shot. I listed the home and we got our buyer an early bird look inside. Interestingly, my buyer decided not to pursue an offer on the house due to possible job relocation, but we sold it to another buyer the first day on the market in a multiple offer situation.*

*Pretty cool huh? I cannot stress enough that after working with hundreds of sellers, I am fully confident that these folks would not have listed the home without having seen our Buyer Listing and the assurance that gave them.*

*That means they would have missed out and continued to stress about the house, dealing with renters and repairs from states away. That's what I call a win-win.*

*Now, back to the first call. Not long after pressing 'send' on the email to my past client with our Buyer Listing info link, I got a call back from her. She was excited to tell me that she'd mentioned it to her co-worker who then made a Facebook post about it because she knew some people that lived in the area.*

*Instantly she got a response from a friend that asked to be put in touch with me because she, too, had moved out of the area, was now renting out the property and wanted to sell.*

*From that morning's prospecting I ended up with TWO SOLD listings and THREE additional seller leads who will be selling in the near future...not to mention the buyer leads we generated from those listings and some new networking connections.*

*Here's the best part: these were not hard sales! I did not have to stalk these sellers and convince them to meet with me. I did not have to hedge out any competing agents or anything like that. In fact, these sellers were stalking me...coming to me and only me.*

I share this story so that you can have a real-world example to relate to as I explain the 3-step process throughout this chapter.

It's the same process I used in the example and have used many times since with very similar outcomes.

## The 3 Steps to Turning Buyers into Listings

### Step 1: Create Buyer Listing

This is where the process has to start. Without having a system to know and track what your buyers (or your team's buyers) are looking for and have that information in a *marketable format*, you can't expect to produce results like those I shared in the example.

Sure, you could call people and say "we have buyers" and leave the specifics out, but you'll soon be wondering why sellers aren't lining up at your door. It's not real to them.

They've probably heard that before. A specific Buyer Listing makes it real.

**Example of a Buyer Listing on MyBuyerListing.com**

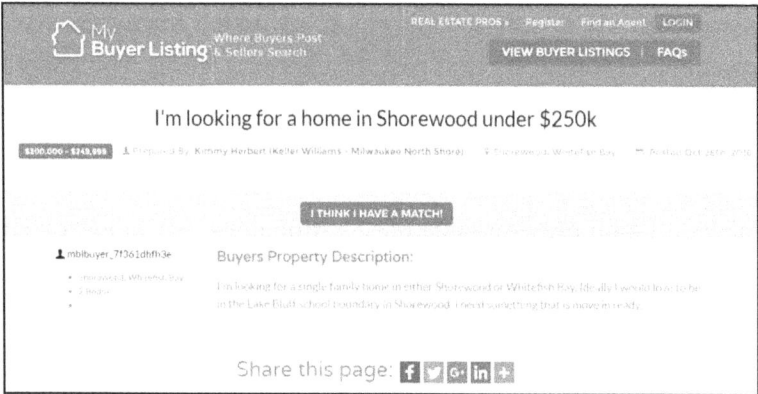

This example fits the definition of Buyer Listings I introduced you to earlier:

**(buy · er  list · ing)**

noun

REAL ESTATE

a *marketable display* of homebuyers' search criteria that when properly marketed *generates leads.*
"buyer listings carry the same marketing and lead generation opportunities as Seller Listings when you have the right systems and strategies."

This is a display (posted, seeable, shareable, informative, live) we can send to people and it offers multiple ways to turn that viewing into an inquiry (lead).

The good news is that you (or a team member) probably already do this step at some level.

Anytime you meet or talk with a buyer and you jot down their search criteria in a notebook or on an intake form, you have essentially created the first part of a Buyer Listing. The second step is putting it into a *marketable format.* Now it's about doing it with a bigger vision and purpose in mind.

What's the number one rule for creating a Buyer Listing? Get it on paper and out of the brain file. *Storing it in your head doesn't count.* If you're on a team, get it where everyone can see it.

Now it's about doing something with it that creates new business opportunities, which brings us to step number two.

**Step 2: Share Your Buyer Listings with the World**

Here is where most agents are missing out on HUGE opportunity. They are already creating a basic form of a Buyer Listing, but then it stays in the file, on your desk or on the backend of a listing cart in your website's database.

To me, now that I know the power of Buyer Listings, this is just like signing a new seller listing and leaving all the paperwork in the file, never telling anyone about it, not marketing it, not putting it in the MLS system, keeping it off the hundreds of different websites out there, not posting your newest gem on your Facebook feed, no sign in the yard, no open house...

nothing.

If that's what we did with seller listings we certainly wouldn't expect to sell it, much less produce additional leads from it.

In fact, treating a seller listing like that would be unfathomable. You probably cannot comprehend *not* doing your due diligence with marketing it, because that's just what you do with listings, right?

Adopt the same mindset for Buyer Listings.

> Now that you know their power, treat Buyer Listings the same as your seller listings.

Buyer Listings should be treated no differently than seller listings now that you have an understanding of the power they hold. Up until now you got a buy because no one had introduced you to these strategies, but today is a new day.

So, *sharing your Buyer Listings with the world* is about taking a buyer's search criteria (that you already have in a file) and creating a Buyer Listing and letting as many people as possible know about it.

Get your Buyer Listings into a shareable format.

There are as many strategies for marketing Buyer Listings as there are seller listings...too many to cover in detail in this book. Here are a few examples, and if you want to learn more, access our entire training vault—including one-on-one and group strategy sessions, coaching and many more resources—at MyBuyerListing.com/agent-info.

### Examples of Buyer Listing Marketing Strategies

1. Direct mail
2. Social media
3. Facebook ads and posts
4. Database drip campaigns
5. Past clients
6. Open Houses
7. Expireds
8. Door knocking
9. Circle prospecting
10. Website call to action link
11. FSBO's
12. Lead conversion – buyers and sellers

The key is to get your Buyer Listings out there in front of as many homeowners and people as possible so they come back to you as seller leads and inquiries.

With Buyer Listings, you've got a very compelling message to share that homeowners want to know more about.

Of course you can't share the Buyer Listing until you first create it in step one – it's a process, just like most things that are worthwhile.

Having an efficient system that allows you to do this regularly is vital, and we'll get into that in just a bit.

First, I want to cover the nearly "magical" third step. I say *nearly* magical because there is nothing truly magical about it, other than the result it produces when you follow it feels like unicorn sparkles and pots of gold.

**Step 3: Follow Up with a Visual Buyer Listing**

By following up with a visual Buyer Listing you're simply *sending some sort of visual representation of your buyer's search criteria that your prospects or the people you had a conversation with can interact with and retain.*

Why? I'll give you an example. In chapter 3 I mentioned the neighborhood that I was prospecting in the first time I called around with a Buyer Listing. Do you remember the name of it?

If you do you should probably be in a memory competition somewhere. Chances are good that by now the name has escaped you. Don't feel bad, it just means you're like the rest of us, including the people you market and prospect to.

This world we live in is more distracting than ever, people are busier than ever and we are presented with more ads, messages, offers and information than ever.

How can you make yours stick and give it a shelf life? The best way to be memorable is to follow up with a visual.

If you recall the example I shared earlier, each time I talked with someone about our Buyer Listings I followed up by sending them an email with a link to the Buyer Listing.

As they read it, it becomes real and they can visualize a real buyer behind it. It also gives them a visual; the opportunity to picture a house they may know of...*like the one I was in last month, and oh yeah, the owner just got a job transfer...*

Following up with a visual allows people time to think, otherwise there's too much of a chance to get brushed off with everything else and get lost in the noise.

### If You Share it, They Will Come

The best news is that people love looking over Buyer Listings just like people love looking at houses for sale even when they aren't buying. They send them around to friends, family and co-workers, share them on their Facebook page and every now and then decide it's time to move. All those are winning situations for you and can be done easily with your Buyer Listings.

So whether you send it in the mail, email, text or whatever, make sure you're always following up with a visual and your efforts will be richly rewarded.

Check out the system we've constructed for you at MyBuyerListing.com/agent-info. It makes it super simple to follow up with a visual for an individual Buyer Listing or an entire list in seconds and through a variety of media and print.

Even if the initial offer or message was visual, I still send out another visual whenever someone inquires or we have a conversation.

## It's Who You Know

Now you have the three steps to turn buyers into listings.

There's one more thing about my earlier example I'd like to share with you, and I think will really help this sink in.

I learned the hard way that when it comes to building a business, tapping into your existing network of people who already know and like you is valuable. When I got started in real estate I skipped over this and went straight for *cold* business.

> Because I shared my Buyer Listings with her, she had the tool to connect me with a seller.

When I started Buyer Listing marketing, having learned my lesson, I started with my warm people. In fact, I started with the warmest of them all...my mother.

I talk to my mom almost every day. We spend most Friday evenings with my parents on the back porch while the kids skin their knees on bikes and keep the stain remover companies in business.

Mom has been a great referral source and client over the years and knows that I'm always looking to connect with new clients. I have no bigger fan than my mother.

However, if I hadn't shared my Buyer Listing with her, she wouldn't have had the tools to connect me with that seller (my mother was the source of the listing referral from the earlier example of my first Buyer Listing marketing activities).

So, a healthy question to ask yourself right now would be:

*How much business do I leave on the table by*
*not sharing my Buyer Listings with people?*

In my experience, it's at least one piece of business for every single buyer.

While that may sting a bit, it should also excite you about the opportunity you have right in front of you to dramatically increase your production with Buyer Listings.

### Exercise

Don't take my word for it, see for yourself.

Call, text or email three of your warmest contacts and ask them if they think it would be interesting to see a list of active homebuyers you're working with and a detailed description of what they are looking for in a home: their desired location, neighborhood, price range, etc.

It could go something like this:

*I'm looking into a new service for my real estate business to better serve our community. Do you think it would be interesting if I were able to send you a list of the buyers I am actively showing properties to and a detailed description of what type of home they are looking for?*

# Chapter 6

## THE STRATEGIES

*"The best content in the world won't drive revenue if nobody sees it."* – Revenue Disruption

*"If you don't have a competitive advantage, don't compete."* – Jack Welch

Hopefully by now you're beginning to discover your hunger for greater results in your real estate business and you know why you want it (affectionately referred to as your WHY). It may not be 100 percent clear yet, but you know you want more. Now we can look at *how* to make that happen.

There are a couple ways to go about creating more. One option would be to double down and increase the volume of the activities you are already doing that drive your results.

For example, if you want to increase your production by 10 percent, it would then take 10 percent more time, 10 percent more expense and 10 percent more of everything else that goes into your previous production. If you worked an average of 40 hours a week this would mean working four additional hours each week to reach your new goal.

The problem with this plan is that unless you were really slacking off prior to now, you may not have the time, energy or resources available to do more or you simply may not want to make that trade off. Let's be real, more time spent in our business means less time for everything (and everyone) else.

This work more strategy may get you by for a while. With improvements in skill, efficiency and systems you can actually run a pretty good growth curve...for a while.

Eventually though, it will catch up to you and you'll hit a ceiling. Let's take that 10 percent example from earlier.

Say you want to increase your production next year by 10 percent. You buckle down, put in the extra work and extra four hours a week, make the extra investments and make it happen. Along the way your skills improve and you find some systems that allow you to increase your efficiency and cut back to 42 hours a week. You reach your new goals...YOU DID IT!

But what happens next year? And the year after that, and five years down the road? This method is not sustainable for continued growth. It is, however, a path to poor self-care and deteriorating relationships.

Unless you're truly a slacker, putting more time in isn't the answer. We need a better lever. We need to work smarter rather than harder.

The second option is to hire someone. This option is fantastic, but brings its own set of challenges. Any inefficiency you had will likely be duplicated in your hires. Likewise, any efficiency you have will be duplicated.

In the coming pages I'll introduce you to simple strategies to set you on that path to maximum efficiency.

There are certainly more strategies you can implement when it comes to Buyer Listings, but these are likely to be your best leverage, producing the most results with the least amount of your time or energy.

There is only one that you need to get started.

### STRATEGY 1 – The Foundational Strategies of MyBuyerListing.com

Once you have a list of your buyers' search criteria compiled somewhere, easily shareable (we'll get to the how of that soon…), here's the first strategy for how to use it. This strategy has two parts and is designed to help you get your Buyer Listings out to a broad audience on a regular basis. In fact, you can do both parts in as little as five minutes per month when you have the right system.

Keep in mind, these next strategies are part of the second step in turning buyers into listings, which is "Share your Buyer Listings with the World," and can only occur after you've completed the first step ("Create a Buyer Listing").

### The Delivery

The first part is a monthly social media post where you share your Buyer Listing link with your audience. Create a short post informing your audience that you're actively showing properties to home buyers (just like how you share links to the list of properties you have for sale). This peaks your audience's interest in an entirely new way, and they see you're actively working your business.

The second part is to send your database a monthly update of buyers you're showing properties to. Type up a short email with your Buyer Listing link asking if they know of anyone this month who may have a suitable property or if they have a particular type of home you should be keeping your radar tuned in for them.

Once it's in their inbox (or on their favorite social media platform), they can use the link to view details about the buyers you're working with in an interactive way, request more information and they can share your list with others if they so choose. All winning propositions for you!

When you consistently do this you'll be teaching your audience two things: you are always meeting new home buyers and looking for additional properties to show them (seller magnet), and you're proactive in creating opportunities for your buyers that extends beyond homes actively *on the market* (buyer magnet).

Any homeowner who is considering selling their home finds these qualities attractive and it provides great incentive for them to contact you first when they are considering making a move.

Your buying audience will see that you're proactive in helping your buyer clients find the ideal property. It shows them you won't just put them on an automatic listing cart and hope the right home comes along. It shows them how you go above and beyond and buyers really appreciate that. Their biggest concern is finding a home that fits their needs and this strategy is a great way to *show* them how you do that.

## The Goal

By simply putting your Buyer Listings out into the world you generate inquiries from interested parties and give your audience the ability to share your list with others, too, thereby extending your natural reach.

Just imagine if you were a homeowner and for the past three months, six months or five years you had received a monthly update from a real estate agent about home buyers they were showing properties to. Wouldn't you call that person immediately when you were considering a move? The answer is yes, and most importantly the answer is yes for many of the homeowners in your market.

When someone requests more information about a particular buyer there's a high likelihood that they have an interest in selling their home and *you* are now in a conversation with them.

That's the long and the short of it. Buyer Listings empower valuable conversations.

These conversations are not limited to inquiries from potential sellers. You'll end up with all manner of comments and inquiries. You'll very likely have random people respond with comments along the lines of, *do you know of any 4 bedroom houses with a finished basement*?

*Yes, yes I do…*

Now you have a conversation open with a likely buyer. Or, it may just be someone responding with, *this is really cool*. In that case you have a great opportunity to see if they have any upcoming real estate plans or if they know of anyone else that may be interested in seeing a list of active buyers (any potential sellers they may know) or someone that would benefit from your proactive approach in finding off-market properties (buyer referrals).

In each case, you've differentiated yourself to your audience with a unique value proposition and helped cement in their minds that *you* are the agent of choice in your market.

These two strategies, a monthly email and social media post with your Buyer Listing link, are foundational and where we recommend starting, and for good reason.

### All Roads Lead to One

Not only are monthly emails and social media posts extremely time-leveraged and two of the most efficient ways to get your Buyer Listings out into the world, as you now know, they come back as leads for new business opportunities. They are also the point that all the other strategies you employ will come back to.

The two foundational strategies enable you to have a long term communication plan of highly exclusive, highly relevant and highly interesting content. By having the foundational strategies in place you now have the ability to offer, to virtually anyone in your marketplace, the chance to receive this information.

That becomes the next step: building a list of subscribers who receive your monthly Buyer Listing updates.

## Ensuring a Strong Foundation

To make sure that your Buyer Listing message and offer is delivered on a consistent basis there are a few additional thoughts I want to share with you.

In order for these strategies to work we have to remind ourselves to do it.

Pick a day of the month that you want to make your Buyer Listing social media post and make a recurring event on your calendar.

Likewise, do the same thing for the monthly email. Or if you really want to leverage this strategy, set up an automated campaign in your email system so that it goes out each and every month without even having to think about it. This is obviously the preferred method.

The MyBuyerListing.com resource guide is full of email templates and sample social media posts so that you don't have to build yours from scratch. Literally copy and paste our proven content into your own campaign.

Find these templates in our Training and Resource Center page once you've set up your agent account at: MyBuyerListing.com/ agent-info.

## Exercise

Set a timer, go to your favorite social media site and make a post.

How long did it take? _____ minutes

When you have a MyBuyerListing.com link, sharing your Buyer Listings is that quick and easy.

We've had members report getting their first lead from their Buyer Listings within minutes of making their first post even with sending out just a single Buyer Listing.

# Chapter 7

# STRATEGY – DOOR OPENER OFFER

*"The doors we open and close each day decide the lives we live."*
– Flora Whittemore

*"I think a simple rule of business is, if you do the things that are
easier first, then you can actually make a lot of progress."*
– Mark Zuckerberg

In the last chapter I introduced you to the foundational strategies at the core of effectively marketing your Buyer Listings to generate new business.

As we move along, the strategies will get slightly more involved and complex, although all of them are relatively easy to implement.

In following that sequence, the next strategy I want to introduce to you is what I call the Door Opener.

> A great offer is relevant, unique and in alignment with the purpose you have in making it.

The essence of this strategy is to simply start talking to people about your Buyer Listings and offer to send them regular updates.

Every offer must have two parts: the actual offer itself and the deliverable. The key in having a great offer is that it has to be relevant, unique and in alignment with the purpose you have in making it.

The key for the deliverable is that it needs to be *efficient* and *valuable*.

For example, we could offer to send home improvement tips to our database, which many agents do. While this may be relative to our audience, when it comes to being unique and in alignment with our purpose in making it, I'm not so sure. In that case, aren't we really branding ourselves more as a "Bob Villa" than a dynamite real estate agent?

I mean think about it...when was the last time someone hired you because their friend told them you have the best home maintenance tips? Uh, never!

Buyer Listings allow you to make *better offers* and deliver *better content* that is *better aligned* with our purpose as a real estate agent. Please hear me, I'm not saying home maintenance tips are bad. I'm saying a regular update of your Buyer Listings is better, more relevant and will bring you better results.

The offer is actually the easy part. It's the deliverable that more often creates a bit of a challenge. The challenge is once we have made an offer (*would you like to receive these updates?*) and it's been accepted (*sure!*), we then have to deliver. This involves some work on our end. If we offer to send a home valuation or market updates, we have to compile those reports or have a system that does it for us.

A great offer has a leveraged deliverable – especially if it's an offer you'll be making to lots of people. A leveraged deliverable means it takes a minimal amount of time and effort to deliver what you said you would, yet is still valuable to the recipient.

> A *leveraged deliverable* is valuable, yet takes you a minimal amount of time and effort to deliver it.

Buyer Listings meet all the criteria of a great offer: simple for you, interesting for readers.

As a tool, MyBuyerListing.com is an excellent way for you to deliver it efficiently – simply share your link or quickly add someone to your monthly Buyer Listing email group.

So, now that you have a great offer (a list of active homebuyers) and a system for delivery, it's time to start opening doors for people.

### Door Opener

In this strategy you will take advantage of those moments of opportunity surrounding each of us every day to make an offer to someone and bring them into your world.

Specifically, you will be making an offer to send people a list of your Buyer Listings.

Who will you be making this offer to? Well, if you want to really leverage your life and business the simple answer is...*everyone.*

You'll offer to send your list of active buyers to the person next to you in line at Starbucks. You'll offer it to your barber when you go in for a trim, you'll offer it out to the other spectators at your kids soccer game, to people at a holiday party, neighbors, etc.

You see, generating business opportunities doesn't have to be an isolated event separate from the rest of your life and business. It can actually, and should be, woven right into the everyday conversations and opportunities that surround us all the time.

You're not really having to do much "more" to put this strategy in play, you're simply going to add a piece to the conversations you're having everyday by saying:

### Door Opener Script

*"I have several home buyers who I'm currently showing properties to, and I'd love to send you a list that details the types of properties they're looking for...that way if you ever had a need to sell or know of any friends or family members that need a buyer for their home, you'll have my list! Plus it's pretty cool to see what home buyers are actively looking for in the area. Sounds pretty interesting, doesn't it?"*

They will most likely say yes to this, and then you simply say:

*"Great, I'll send you a link so you can see the list and all the details. What's the best email address for you? Since I'm always meeting new buyers, I'll update you from time to time with what we're out searching for...won't that be great?"*

As you talk with people, keep a notebook handy or use your

phone to take down their email addresses.

## The Goal

That short, simple little script is the best tool I know of for adding people to your database. Once they say yes, you simply *add them to your email list of people who receive your monthly Buyer Listing updates.*

It was impressed on me very early in my real estate career just how important building a database was to the health of my business.

The thing I always struggled with was figuring out what I could offer to a wide range of people that would be of enough value for them to say yes and give me their contact information.

I found my answer with Buyer Listings and this very script, and I hope you will, too. Even if they don't own a home or have no immediate real estate plans, the nature of the offer and content has proven irresistible to most people. I consistently get a yes with 8 out of 10 strangers and receive their contact information.

This is a far better outcome than any other offer I've made where my ratio would tend to be the exact opposite – maybe two yes's out of ten, regardless of what I was offering. You can offer it over the phone or in person, it doesn't matter, and that's the beauty.

You now have the offer, deliverable and the script to turn nearly every conversation into a business-building opportunity (with a better offer than you may have had before).

Keep in mind that each conversation you have and each *yes* is much bigger than what's on the surface. When you have these conversations and send your list out to more and more people, many will pass the list on to places you weren't able to reach by yourself.

If you build a database of 100 recipients and 10 of them decide to forward it on to 10 others, your efforts and reach doubled without any additional work on your part. Weave this into your conversations and watch your business soar.

Now you get to make a decision: will you or won't you?

I am reminded of a quote from Jim Rohn, who has been a key influence on my life through his birds and bees way of looking at life's challenges and its opportunities.

> *"The things that are easy to do are easy not to do."*
> – Jim Rohn

The difference between whether you will or you won't, will be the results you get to experience. If you've invested the time and energy in reading to this point, I hope you'll take that next step and put it to use.

## Exercise

If you haven't already done so, I invite you to visit MyBuyerListing.com/agent-info to explore our solutions and see how agents across the country are using them to propel their businesses forward.

# Chapter 8

# STRATEGY – OPEN HOUSES

*"If you want something you've never had, you must be willing to do something you've never done."*
– Thomas Jefferson

*"Every time you are tempted to react in the same old way, ask if you want to be a prisoner of the past or a pioneer of the future."*
– Deepak Chopra

There was a point in my business where I was doing an open house seven days a week. Yep, you heard me right. I would host them at 5:00 p.m. during weeknights in high traffic areas to take advantage of commuter traffic, and then noon on Saturday and the traditional Sunday from 2-4 (sometimes I would split this time and do two separate houses, one hour each). Remember, I told you about the one where I was in a dunk tank and our guests (more than 75 registrations) got the chance to take their best shot. Thank God it was a hot, summer day in Illinois!

Open houses were the primary source not only for capturing immediate business but also for adding people to my database. I recall one open house that yielded me four listings within one block of the house I was holding open.

It's fair to say that I love open houses for building a real estate business.

They were not always productive for me though. I had to go through a learning curve to produce those kinds of results. You see, at first I had a faulty view of what an open house was supposed to be. That view determined my strategy and as a consequence, my open house strategy didn't work well (this applies to Buyer Listings, too).

In the beginning I had some open houses where no one came. What a waste of my precious time. Luckily I got introduced to a new viewpoint and a few simple strategies I could employ to turn my stagnant open houses into bustling events and lead-generation machines.

I learned how to host a purposeful open house from Chris Suarez (who teaches "Hold it Open and Close the Deal" for MAPS Coaching) and I'm forever grateful for his willingness to share his success secrets and strategies.

My results from open houses not only improved but I began to see how making a simple tweak here and there could dramatically impact results...something I've constantly explored and the only reason this book exists.

> I began to see how making simple tweaks here and there could dramatically impact results.

This strategy is one of those tweaks that will dramatically improve the results you get from open houses if you're already hosting them and if you're not, may make you want to start.

### At the Open House

The date and time for your open house is set and it's official that you will be spending a chunk of your life there. Since you're going to be there anyway, let's talk about how to get the most out of it.

There are really three stages to an open house: before, during and after. In this strategy we'll focus on the *during* and *after* stages.

At the open house I believe there are three basic things you want to accomplish:

1) Capture the contact information from the guests so you can follow up.

2) Find out at least one thing that is important to each guest.

3) Differentiate yourself and the services you offer from "the crowd."

Adding your Buyer Listing value proposition will help you accomplish all three.

### Registration – Value for Sellers

To start, let's look at the registration process. You really want people to register at the open house feeling like they got value for doing it, not that they were forced to. Since we are trying to make a connection and build a relationship with each guest this is very important.

Enter your Buyer Listing offer…

In this strategy, all you will be doing is bringing two additional forms with you to your open house.

The first is a sign-in sheet to get your active buyer list. For the second form, take your regular sign-in sheet (template available in the MyBuyerListings.com Training and Resource Center after signing up), paste one of your Buyer Listings at the top and make the headline:

**I may already have a buyer for your home.
Sign up to get a list of active buyers I'm currently
showing properties to.**

Since many of your open house guests are sellers in disguise, this will help you identify who those people are. Even if they're looking to buy the home, it's likely they may need to sell one first.

This form also accomplishes all three basic things we want to accomplish at the open house. First, we got their contact information, and since they registered for something they really want, you're likely to get better contact information. Second, we found out something important to them, in this case, getting a list of active home buyers. Now we can deliver something of value in our follow up. Finally, you definitely set yourself apart with this type of unique offer. If they visit five other open houses that day, it's very likely you'll be the only one offering a list of active buyer details.

### Registration – Value for Buyers

You see how to appeal to the sellers that attend your open

houses, now let's look at how to cater to the buyers.

For buyers, the value proposition is that you have a *unique service* that doesn't limit them to homes that are actively for sale.

Delivering this to buyers is easy. Make a flyer illustrating your Buyer Marketing Service and a form they can fill out with their basic home search criteria (flyer examples are available in MyBuyerListing.com's Training Center).

This is so effective because you're opening up a much bigger world for these prospective buyers. If you simply ask for their home search criteria and offer to send them property alerts, then you're not offering anything unique that they can't get themselves from hundreds of different sources (in many cases, they already have a new listing alert set up somewhere).

Again, by adding this one additional form and offer, you'll be accomplishing the three basic goals of your open house for the buyers that show up.

*You can get all the forms needed for your open house at MyBuyerListing.com Training and Resource Center after setting up your agent account.*

### After the Open House – Follow Up

In my opinion, where the open house *ends* is where the bulk of opportunity for you *begins*.

Here's the challenge with open houses: you have a very limited amount of time to interact with your guests. Converting your open house guests into clients is all about the follow up.

After the open house add all the guests who signed up to receive your buyer list to your monthly Buyer Listing update email list.

> Where the open house ends is where the bulk of opportunity for you begins.

Next, call them to make sure they received it and start asking questions to find out what their future plans are and why they were interested in a list of active buyers. The goal here is to qualify them and get them into your office for an appointment.

That call could go something like this:

*"Did you receive the active buyer list I sent to you after the open house?"*

*"Did you see any buyers who looked like they could be a match for your home?"*

*"When do you need to move by?"*

*"What's prompting your move?"*

*"I meet with new buyers all the time. If you share some details with me about your home, I can keep my eyes and ears open for one that would be a match for your home. When would be a good time to get together so I can learn more about your home? I can also prepare a comprehensive marketing plan and home value report for you after that meeting to make sure your upcoming move is a smooth one."*

Most agents will lead with the appointment offer or home valuation. The problem is *most* agents lead with that. If you do the same, you'll be the same as every other agent in the mind of this prospect.

When you employ this new twist, you are different in their minds and your results will speak to it.

For your guests who filled out the Buyer Listing criteria form, I still recommend adding them to your monthly Buyer Listing update email list. You never know who they know and there's still a good chance they're a seller in disguise. Doing this will also further illustrate that you're proactive in finding your buyers the best house to fit their needs.

The follow up call to potential buyers will be a bit different and will follow this line of questions:

*"Are you interested in having more property options available than just the small percentage actively for sale?"*
*"When do you need to move by?"*
*"What's prompting your move?"*
*"I'd like to get a better understanding of what you desire for your new home so I can focus my efforts in the right area. Since I'll be doing a lot more than just setting you up with an automatic property search this is really important. When would you be available to come in and review some sample properties together so I can start lining up some additional option for you?"*

Most agents will lead with an offer to set up "instant property alerts" or the offer to have them come in for a consultation. Just like with sellers you followed up with, lead with something more unique and more valuable. Buyers love nothing more than the idea of getting the first crack at an off-market property, so you'll definitely accomplish that while also differentiating yourself.

### Follow Up – Getting Your Next Listing

This part of your open house strategy is the icing on the cake, the cherry on top and the tipping point all rolled into one.

You met buyers at the open house, and if you did the right things you should now have some new Buyer Listings for at least some of the guests.

With this part of the strategy you can now leverage those Buyer Listings to get your next seller listing in the same neighborhood.

To do this, simply go back to the neighborhood you just did the open house in and reach out to the neighbors with the following proposition:

*"I just hosted an open house in your neighborhood and I met several buyers that are interested in moving into your area but that particular house wasn't quite the right fit for them. I promised them I would reach out to the neighbors to see if there was anyone else in the neighborhood that would consider selling. Could I send you a list of what these buyers are looking for, so that if you or anyone you know in the area is thinking of moving, you can see if I might already have a buyer ready to go. It's also pretty interesting to see what active buyers are looking for in your area."*

Whoa…I still get chills every time I share this and I hope you just did too.

You can deliver this offer by door knocking, phone calls or even direct mail. If you door knock, take one copy of your Buyer Listings list to show them and (of course) offer to send them the full list by email. This way you'll be able to add them to your monthly Buyer Listing update email list.

### The Big Picture – Taking Over the Neighborhood

When you go back to the neighborhood after the open house you're not only likely to find an immediate seller lead, you are building your database for that area.

Let's say you host an open house at house A and do the follow up activities. You add 15 people in that area to your monthly Buyer Listing update email. You also got a new listing from those activities and put house B on the market the next month. At that point you repeat the process and hold house B open…getting even more Buyer Listings. Then, you go back to the neighborhood and add another 15 to your database and monthly Buyer Listing update email. The first 15 from house A get your monthly Buyer Listing update email showing the new buyers you met at house B, in addition to sending it to the new group.

Now 30 people in the neighborhood are on your list seeing your signs and getting a monthly email with buyers looking in their area. Continue this process and it won't be long before you dominate the mindshare and market share for that area. Each time you go out and add people to your list it gets easier and easier.

The key in this strategy is to focus on doing open houses in areas where you want more business and that have a good turnover rate. If you don't have a listing in those areas, offer to host an open house for an agent who does to get the process started.

**Exercise**

What neighborhood would you like to grow your business in?

Are you willing to invest at least 10 minutes of prep and 1 hour of post open house activity to build your market share there?

Yes/No

If you answered *yes,* come on board and we will help get you started at *MyBuyerListing.com/agent-info.*

## Chapter 9

## STRATEGY – FSBO

Often referred to by real estate agents as the Fastest Source of Business Opportunity, For Sale by Owner properties (FSBO's) are an interesting beast.

On one hand, these homeowners have already decided they want to sell their home at some level and have made that information publically available.

> Your job is to stand out from the crowd if you want to bring on clients.

Consequently, they are easy to find and get in touch with, so that makes our job of identifying people with a desire to sell relatively easy.

On the other hand, at some level they haven't seen the value in hiring a real estate agent to help them through the process.

Where we gain an advantage in one area, we have a bit of a hurdle to overcome in another.

In addition, the minute the homeowner puts an FSBO sign in the yard, you can be sure you'll have competition in retaining them as a client. In many cases they'll be bombarded with calls from agents pursuing them.

Your job is to stand out from that crowd if you wish to bring them on as a client.

There are a few things to be aware of when it comes to FSBO's:

- 88 percent of home buyers made their purchase through a real estate agent.

- 88 percent of FSBO's eventually list with an agent.

- It takes an average of 6-8 weeks for these FSBO's to decide to hire an agent.

Now, I have to ask you a quick question. Have you ever had a buyer client contact an FSBO directly or find an off-market property to purchase? The National Association of Realtors reported that 12 percent of FSBO's sold the home to a buyer that contacted them directly. These buyers were marketing their own Buyer Listing...at least at some level. You want to be the one doing that for them.

We know most FSBO's are eventually going to list with an agent. How do you ensure that it's you?

For many agents, these statistics are nothing new. You already knew them and you already knew that FSBO's are a marathon not a sprint. You already knew they were getting tons of calls from agents.

Here's what you may not have known that I've learned from countless interactions with FSBO's.

They are confused.

They are confused about how to get their home sold. They're

confused about the reality of being able to sell their home on their own. They're confused about the process. Whether they admit it or not, they're confused about some aspect of what their attempting to do. This type of confusion actually helps you build your case...but there is more confusion that's working against you.

FSBO's are confused by why agents are calling them wanting to list their home. They're confused about which agent was which and said what. They're confused thinking that agents that "previewed" their home are going to sell it. They're confused about what to believe and what not to believe.

You may have already found some pretty awesome ways of helping FSBO homeowners sort through it all and in the end, hire you. If so, good for you. This next thought will help even more.

To really win with FSBO's you have to stand out against the noise and confusion and offer things that are valuable to them. That's the simple shift Buyer Listings allow that will dramatically change your FSBO conversion results.

### FSBO's Standing Out Against the Crowd

Most agents are calling and immediately offering to preview the house or pummeling the homeowner with stats that that support the fact that there's a slim chance they'll be successful on their own. Basically starting a conversation with a perfect stranger by telling them they're wrong...not what I would call planting the seeds of a lasting relationship.

In this strategy you are going to be different than them. In the first call you make to an FSBO you'll simply say:

*"I noticed you have your house for sale and wanted to send you over a list of the home buyers I'm currently showing properties to and see if any sound like they might be a good match for your house."*

Then, stop and listen…

They'll say yes to this in nearly every case and now you've already distanced yourself from every other agent that has called or will call in the future. You're *that helpful agent* and a breath of fresh air.

While you're on the phone ask a few more simple qualifying questions like:

*"Where are you planning on moving to?"*
*"When do you want to be moved by?"*

You're only going to mention the option of meeting with you if they give some indication that they're open to it.

This may seem counterintuitive and contradictory to the typical approach with FSBO's and that is by design. By actually being less aggressive you help the owner keep an open mind with you and give them the chance to trust you.

Send over your Buyer Listing link as soon as you get off the phone. Be sure to add them to your list to get your monthly Buyer Listing update email as well so they get it every month from then on.

Call them the next day to see if they've had a chance to review the list and if any buyers look like a possible match.

It really doesn't matter whether or not you had any buyers on your list that match their home. If not simply say:

*"Okay, no worries. Sounds like I still need to find you one then, huh?"*

*"I meet with new buyers all the time. It will be a bit tough for me to highlight your property to them without having seen it. Would it be possible to swing by and take a look this week?"*

Again, they are very likely to say yes to this. You may be thinking, this has become the normal approach but now a step behind everyone else who's already offered to do that…but trust me, you're not. I can promise you that you will have much better rapport built up by sending the Buyer List in the beginning, and the homeowner will be more receptive to what you have to share from here on out.

You gave them your list which was honest, generous and helpful, and that goes a long way. Those agents that claimed to have a possible buyer, previewed the home, and launched right into a listing presentation have likely distanced themselves.

Once they've agreed to have you come by, again be transparent. *"Would it be helpful for you if I brought a detailed report of recent sales activity for your neighborhood with me?"*

Again, you'll get another yes here.

*"While I'm there, I'd love to share some tips with you on how we find buyers and some ways I can be most effective in finding one for your house."*

Schedule a time to stop by and preview the house. While you're previewing, ask questions.

Then, sit down and go over your market report.

This will lead you into discussing how buyers find and select properties and how you can best assist in finding a buyer for their home (which happens to be by marketing it). Since you have asked questions, you'll know their motivating factors and what's giving them challenges.

Your only job at this point is to offer solutions to make the challenges go away and get them to what is motivating them.

Now it's appropriate to share the statistics that show the reality of FSBO success rates and how agent-assisted sales typically sell for higher prices, so it really isn't costing them anything to hire you…someone they now trust.

If they don't list with you right away they may still not be willing to accept reality. What we need to understand is that sometimes it just takes time and them experiencing the reality before they believe it.

The key is to not push so hard that you're no longer in the running when the time comes. Remain the helpful agent who is honest and has that neat list of buyers...

It's a delicate balance, but as long as you keep in touch consistently and keep providing value you're in a good spot. I recommend calling to check in at least once a week and offer something of value each time.

You already added them to your Buyer Listing update email list which will continue to build credibility and value.

**FSBO – Buyer Listing Approach**

If in your conversation with the homeowner you find out that they'll be purchasing a new home in your market, you have another great opportunity to build value and rapport with them. They may not know that as a buyer, there's no fee for them to work with you.

Too many agents miss out on this opportunity and only focus on the listing.

With this approach you're still going to do everything in the previous steps. In addition, once you have sent the buyer list you will offer to create a Buyer Listing for *them* and begin marketing it to find the ideal home for them to move into. Chances are you're probably the only one who has offered this type of service to them, so they'll likely say yes.

As you take them under your wing as a buyer, they get to experience your service and the relationship builds.

Nothing will change a FSBO's motivation faster than finding

that perfect *next home*. You take them through it and they come out saying something like, "Okay, we have to get this house, what's it going to take to get ours sold?"

All the heavy lifting just got done for you.

The reason this is so effective is because people will always give more credibility to what you can *show* them verses what you can *tell* them. When they can actually experience it (in this case, your service) for themselves, you remove all the question marks.

I think you'll not only find this approach to FSBO's refreshing and less stressful, but the results you experience will tell its success story.

Like most of the strategies I'm sharing with you in this book, it won't require a massive overhaul of your current process…just a small tweak here and there to produce a dramatically better result. It's all about efficiency!

You may be like many agents I've met who aren't super excited about approaching FSBO's. This is usually due to a fear of rejection or not being comfortable with the traditional approaches. This strategy not only *feels* very helpful, it *is* very helpful and some of my best clients and biggest advocates today started as FSBO's. To get to that point takes the right approach.

*Note: The FSBO process covered here can also be applied (with a few slight modifications) to expired and withdrawn properties for similarly awesome results!*

# Chapter 10

# HOW BUYER LISTINGS BENEFIT BUYERS

*"Normality is a paved road: it's comfortable to walk but no flowers grow."* –Vincent van Gogh

*"You can be so bad at so many things...and as long as you stay focused on how you're providing value to your users and customers, and you have something that is unique and valuable...you get through all that stuff."*
–Mark Zuckerberg

The benefits of Buyer Listings are widespread when it comes to generating seller leads. Most of this book and the strategies I cover are focused to that end.

It would be remiss, however, to not illustrate the wide appeal and benefits that Buyer Listings have on connecting with and serving home buyers.

The benefit of generating seller leads by marketing Buyer Listings is actually a residual effect of providing a unique and highly valuable service to your home buyer clients.

By delivering this service you'll not only be better equipped to create raving fans out of your home buyer clients, but you'll also attract more of the same.

You'll do it by giving them exactly what they value.

## The Home Buyer Value Proposition

Buyers have many options when it comes to selecting an agent to work with to purchase a home. The focus of this chapter is to make it easy for them to decide to work with *you* by offering a truly unique service, satisfying a craving every home buyer shares.

A home buyer's core objective: get the most of what they want/need in a home for the best price.

Along the way to completing this objective, they expect the process to be accomplished and accompanied by great service, communication, care, etc.

Buyer Listings provide a unique tool that allows you to satisfy both expectations. In short, buyers love Buyer Listings and what they represent.

Typically, to describe the value we provide to buyers it may include things like:

1) Instant property alerts
2) Great communication
3) Superior service
4) Education about the process
5) Negotiations
6) Referrals to other reputable service providers

These are all excellent and essential to creating a great experience for your clients. They just aren't unique...and miss out on one of the most meaningful ways you can provide value to your buyers.

With Buyer Listings you create more opportunities for your buyers to get the most of what they really want: an awesome house at an awesome price.

> Buyer Listings help your buyers get more of what they really want: an awesome house at an awesome price.

You expand their search from the small percentage of homes actively for sale to (potentially) every home in your market.

By creating a Buyer Listing for your clients and actively marketing it, you're going above and beyond what most buyers expect and what most agents provide. Exciting!

It is an awesome conversation that goes something like this:

*"Mr. or Mrs. Buyer,*
*....I'm sure you have noticed that most agents only market their seller listings. One of the advantages you get when you, hire me, is that I actually provide the same level of service to both sellers and buyers. As a buyer I will create an advertisement for you that's based on your specific needs and wants in your new home... Then, I will proactively work to find the very best fit for your new home, including homes that are not even on the market currently. Best of all, this additional service doesn't cost you anything. Would you like to make sure you have the very best options available, or are you okay with seeing what pops up...?"*

In this short illustration, it's easy to see how you will undoubtedly set yourself apart in the eyes of the buyer and connect your service to what they value most.

You can deliver this message (or a similar version – it may need slight modification depending on the situation) in a buyer consultation, over the phone with buyer call-ins, in an email campaign, as a call-to-action on your website, or anywhere else you communicate with potential buyers.

When you do this, the benefits abound.

Your new buyer clients will love you and be much more likely to refer you additional business.

By clearly illustrating the value you provide and how it's unique, you also give your clients and networks the ability to communicate and share it with others.

Buyer Listings make your job of attracting buyer leads, converting those leads into appointments and turning those appointments into *loyal clients*, easier and more effective.

Finally, you also get the residual benefits of proactively serving your buyer clients at the highest level. As you market their Buyer Listing you generate new leads for your business.

Everyone wins.

Best of all, you did it by delivering exceptional value across the board.

## Same Situation – Different Results

Earlier I shared the story of the first listing I took from marketing Buyer Listings.

We were proactively marketing our Buyer Listings to create more opportunities for our clients and were successful in doing so.

The interesting thing is that as soon as the listing went active I had a barrage of agents calling to schedule showings and they all shared a similar story:

*"These buyers have just been waiting for a home like this to hit the market."* Several of the agents also mentioned the fact that their client had already missed out on other listings in the neighborhood that sold immediately.

Could they have secured that listing? Sure, but here's the difference:

Only *one* of us was marketing our Buyer Listings.

Those particular sellers had wanted to sell for years and any of those other agents had the same opportunity to offer the right value which would have triggered them to take action.

In fact, those weren't the only "sellers" in the neighbor-hood. We listed a series of nearly identical homes that were in extremely high demand from our Buyer Listing marketing activities, while everyone else anxiously watched the MLS.

As we continued our buyer marketing efforts, this same scenario repeated itself over and over again.

We did not *create* the inventory for our clients, it was already there. We just found it.

Your market is the same way, regardless of the economy, demand or any other factor. There are always homeowners ready willing and able to sell who will step forward, given the right trigger.

Buyer Listings have proven themselves to me over and over again to be a most effective trigger.

The most interesting part to me is that being proactive about marketing Buyer Listings actually makes things easier, takes less time and generates new business opportunities.

Consider the previous example. In certain cases those agents had written multiple offers for their clients, agonized over the lack of suitable properties and had to console their clients when yet another opportunity was missed.

That's not only hard work...it's no fun at all.

On the flipside, we got to call our buyers and say, "We found it."

There is work in both scenarios, yes. One, however, comes with clear benefits for you, your buyer and a seller. Market your Buyer Listings and your wins will be multiplied.

## Own Your Value – Do it Right

Marketing your Buyer Listings is an awesome thing to do for your clients. Be sure to let them know that you are doing it!

Showing them will take it one step further and put you even further down the road to your next raving fan.

The worst thing you could do with an effective buyer marketing campaign is keep it a secret from your clients. Explain the benefit they are getting and reaffirm their decision to work with you.

I never get tired of hearing stories from our members about how appreciative their clients are that they provide this type of service, and you deserve to hear that, too!

If you really want to build insane momentum, take it a step further and get your clients involved in your buyer marketing.

The script goes like this:

*"One of the reasons we're able to help our clients win is we work as a team. Just like you, we have other buyers looking to find their dream home. We ask each of our clients to share our buyer list with their network in case you know of someone that has the perfect home for one of our other clients and we ask them to do the same for you."*

With the MyBuyerListing.com solution, this can be as easy as them sharing your unique link on their favorite social media pages, getting you out in front of their network in a very powerful way.

Buyer Listings are a part of your marketing, so make sure to be professional with them. Having them in a professional, marketable format helps you share information and capture leads.

I literally think of Buyer Listings and seller listings the same. My rule for Buyer Listings is "no cocktail napkins."

If a seller hired me to market their home and my efforts consisted only of a short, haphazard post about it on social media, I'd get fired immediately.

Remember, when done properly, marketing Buyer Listings isn't a one-time event. It is a process done consistently over time, yielding a high return while delivering exceptional value.

Have a process that's efficient and manageable long term for creating and marketing your Buyer Listings.

## The Magnifying Glass

You've heard the analogy about the sun's energy on a leaf…it produces warmth. But take a magnifying glass and focus that energy, and you can create a very different outcome…FIRE!

Buyer Listings offer the same opportunity for a Real Estate business.

Typically, when I ask an agent how many seller listings they have they can rattle the number off in a heartbeat. When I ask how many active buyers they have (Buyer Listings), I tend to get a much more uncertain response.

Over the years I've watched real estate agents and teams (including my own) create incredible results by focusing on the minimum number of seller listings needed to accomplish a production goal.

That listings-needed number directs all the action and is how agents measure if they're on track. The clarity of hitting a certain number breeds action, momentum and focus.

Buyer Listings bring the same type of clarity to the other half of your business. If it has been unfocused in the past, you can change it today.

Perhaps you're on a team or run a team with agents who work exclusively with buyers. This should be music to their ears.

Many of the buyer agents I've met with over the years have a bit of a disconnect from all the prospecting and lead-generation activities listing agents do; those solely focused on *getting listings.*

Buyer agents get up in the morning to serve their clients and can have a hard time connecting those dots.

When buyer agents have a formidable Buyer Listing and can treat it like a listing agent would for their seller, look out! Now they can prospect relentlessly with a direct benefit to their buyer clients.

Having Buyer Listings brings them greater clarity on where they are in relation to their (and/or team) goals.

Again, everyone wins. They serve their clients at an even higher level and the team benefits from the inevitable listing leads generated from their activities.

**Exercise**

1) List out the top 10 value propositions you currently share with buyers.

2) Put an "E" (expectation) next to the items most buyers would *expect* from any real estate agent. (example – Property Alerts)

3) Put a "C" (common) next to any items that most agents offer. (examples – Great Service, Communication, etc.)

The remaining items are what will separate you in the mind of a client. "E" and "C" are difficult for prospective clients to distinguish between before they've experienced it.

# Chapter 11

# PULLING THE LEVER

*"Give me a lever long enough and a fulcrum on which to place it, and I shall move the world."* – Archimedes

We have explored your WHY behind building a bigger, better business. We have learned a new definition of what a Buyer Listing is and what they can do for your business. You've learned the foundational strategies of how to put your Buyer Listings to work so they come back in the form of new business opportunities.

You have a lever that you didn't have before to create your ideal life and business, if you will apply what you've learned.

Allow me to guide you through the process of turning your new knowledge into simple action to achieve profound results.

## Pulling the Lever

When framing a house, having a pile of 2x4's, a box of nails and a good hammer won't get the job done.

We still have to use the blueprints and do the work to get the end result we desire. The same is true with your Buyer Listings. Simply having them, knowing the strategies and having a blueprint to follow won't do the job of generating a new piece of business for every Buyer Listing.

The only reason we generate leads from our seller listings is because we take action.

The only thing keeping you from producing the same results from your Buyer Listings is taking action and marketing them.

> The only thing keeping you from producing the same results from your Buyer Listings is taking action and marketing them.

This can all change in a matter of minutes by becoming a member at MyBuyerListing.com/agent-info. You can literally set up your agent account, create your first Buyer Listing and make a Facebook post about it in 10 minutes or less.

The lever is there, and all you have to do is pull it by taking the first action step.

One of the great things about our system is the ease of use. You can keep it running in less than five minutes a month. Since I'm an agent myself, I designed it to account for those heavy, busy months when if it wasn't really easy to do, there just wouldn't be time to do it.

The other great thing is that there is no risk. At only $10 a month with no long term contract, if you spend more than a few minutes evaluating and thinking about it, you are losing money and time. Instead of doing that, join our community today and access all the amazing tools we have for you to leverage. We'll walk you right through the getting started process all the way to your first lead. If you're not completely blown away by the end of your orientation, I will happily refund any membership fees you have paid in full.

## The Reality of Doing Something New

There are only so many hours in a day. Right now yours may all be filled and you might be wondering how you can squeeze time for Buyer Listings in.

Even though implementing Buyer Listings is extremely time and cost efficient, especially compared to other marketing and lead generation strategies, this is still a real concern.

One of the primary reasons my business grew from nothing to the top 7 percent in our market in less than three years was because I learned how to evaluate our activities and opportunities and top-grade them quickly.

Sometimes this meant I had to *stop* doing certain things to make room for some-thing better; something better that helped me achieve my goals.

> I had to stop doing certain things in order to make room for something better.

Making room for Buyer Listings was the most productive of these shifts, and I'm confident that it will be for you as well.

To be clear, yes, I am recommending you make room for Buyer Listings, whatever that takes. Not just because I happen to be the founder of MyBuyerListing.com. Creating that site came long after I'd made the decision that Buyer Listings were one of the most efficient ways to generate and convert real estate leads.

I had to then go out and build the system, write the scripts and emails, develop the strategies, test everything and invest significant time and money to have the hammer.

The good news is you don't have to do all that. For just $10 a month you can use the models and systems I've labored on and tested to get there much quicker and easier than I was able to.

I also feel compelled to share with you that when I realized the massive undertaking required to build the site's infrastructure, I decided not to move forward with it. I was busy running my team and serving my clients.

So, I put it on the shelf for nearly a year. As I spent that year doing all my *normal* activities I started feeling a bit insane now knowing there was a better way. I needed this efficient and effective Buyer Listing tool, desperately.

Every conversation I had, every appointment, every lead, I was reminded how crippled my business was by not having the right simple tool available to market Buyer Listings.

That still wasn't enough.

But, I thought about you. I thought about how you may be facing many of the same challenges. I thought about how Buyer Listings could impact your life and business the same way it would mine.

It occurred to me that by developing and sharing these systems and strategies, an agent may be able to make it to one more of their kid's soccer games because they had better control of their business.

The status quo can always be improved.

I thought about our industry and how it's completely changed my life, plus all the great entrepreneurs who've helped me along the way.

In the wake of those additional considerations, I felt my idea transform into a responsibility. My own struggle didn't move me to action. *You* were the tipping point.

So, I began the development process to make this system great for both of us. It's much more than a collection of my ideas, experience and best practices. It is my heart and soul giving back to an industry that has given me so much.

It's a reflection of my belief that no barriers to our best life and business exist except the ones we impose on ourselves.

It's an acknowledgement that the status quo can always be improved, great as it may be.

Getting to where my life, business and MyBuyerListing.com is today has been the most challenging and rewarding journey I've ever been on and it continues as we constantly work to make things better.

What I've learned through this process is when you've decided where you want to go and embark on the journey, the only thing left to do to arrive is *take one more step*. If you follow that formula, you will eventually arrive so long as you apply the lessons learned along the way and make necessary course corrections.

I hope this book has brought value to your life and business and that our paths will cross soon.

My deepest thanks for investing your most valuable resource— *time*—to read it.

This is the last chapter of this book, but I hope it becomes the first chapter in your success story of using Buyer Listings to propel your life and business forward.

Visit MyBuyerListing.com/agent-info to explore our solutions, subscribe to our newsletter and check out my BLOG among all kinds of other cool stuff we've put together for you.

Journey On,

*Brian Inskip*

# ADDITIONAL RESOURCES

Don't let your journey end here, let it begin…
Explore our Revolutionary Real Estate Solutions and
Resources at:

## www.MyBuyerListing.com/agent-info

Get Connected:

facebook.com/BrianInskipJourney
facebook.com/MBLRealEstate
@Mybuyerlisting

BLOG:

## www.MyBuyerListing.com/blog

*also find additional book resources, expanded content and
post your reviews here!

My
**Buyer Listing**

# Training, Speaking and Teaching

Yes, we do:
## Keynote
## Workshops
## Webinars
## Teleconference
## Private Coaching

For more information on bringing Brian to your area for dynamic and mind expanding training or inspiring speaking with his unique blend of practical application visit:

# www.MyBuyerListing.com/bookbrian

My
**Buyer Listing**

# ABOUT THE AUTHOR

Brian Inskip began his real estate career in 2011. A pipefitter, with no college degree, no formal business training and very little capital, he seemed an unlikely candidate for success. Fueled by a passion to provide a better life for his family and make the most out of life, he made a commitment to learn and apply his newfound knowledge and skills.

By the end of his second full year in real estate, Brian had worked his way into the top 7 percent in his market.

Along his journey to Top Producer, Brian began to recognize that his business had a flaw. He realized Buyer Listings present the same types of marketing and lead generation opportunities that seller listings do, but he was letting them go to waste.

Finding no viable tools or training for this type of marketing,

Brian spent the next two years becoming a subject-matter expert and pioneering the strategies and systems agents need to efficiently generate business from Buyer Listings and founded MyBuyerListing.com.

Now he shares his experience, strategies and system with other agents, so they, too, can discover the simple yet powerful benefits that Buyer Listings bring to a real estate agent's business.

Learn more at **www.MyBuyerListing.com/agent-info.**

*Buyer Listing* is proudly published by:

## *Creative Force Press*

www.CreativeForcePress.com

*Do You Have a Book in You?*